Woman
Earth and Spirit

WOMAN
EARTH AND SPIRIT

The Feminine
in Symbol and Myth

HELEN M. LUKE

CROSSROAD · NEW YORK

To all my friends at Apple Farm

ACKNOWLEDGMENTS

The Introduction and "Mother and Daughter Mysteries" are reprinted
from *Parabola* Magazine, Vol. V, no. 4, November, 1980.
Copyright © Society for the Study of Myth and Tradition.

Charles Williams, *Taliessin through Logres*.
London, Oxford University Press, 1954. Used with permission.

1984
The Crossroad Publishing Company
370 Lexington Avenue, New York, NY 10017

Printed in the United States of America

Library of Congress Cataloging in Publication Data

Luke, Helen M., 1904-
Woman: earth and spirit, the feminine in
symbol and myth.

1. Women—Psychology. 2. Women (in religion,
folklore, etc.) 3. Women and religion. 4. Femininity. I. Title.
HQ1206.L843   305.4'2   81-209
ISBN 0-8245-0633-2 (pbk.)   AACR2

Contents

Introduction

One can scarcely open a magazine nowadays—let alone read any of the innumerable brochures announcing lectures, seminars, group therapy, or conferences on psychological matters—without being struck by the preponderance of the theme of the "new woman." When this degree of interest arises we may be sure that it springs from an overwhelming need for a new attitude. As always in the modern world, there is danger that, in the very urgency of that need, the tender new growth of consciousness may be swamped by the spate of theories and opinions poured out upon us.

The safeguard for the individual woman lies in her ability to connect the theories expounded and the emotions aroused in her with her symbolic life; for only when this connection is made do the changes in her actual life become real. Without it, however things may appear on the surface, the theoretical changes merely create a deeper and more destructive conflict in her soul.

Where, however, is a woman to look for nourishment for her inner imagery as her new personality struggles for birth? The changes in the way of Eve have come with staggering swiftness in the last one hundred years, but it seems to me that only recently has the realization broken through that a deeper awareness of the nature of these changes is now essential. If we are to stop the wreckage caused by the disorientation of women, by their loss of identity under the stresses of the new way, then the numinous meaning of the great challenge they face must break through from the unconscious; for no amount of rational analysis can bring healing. Only so can the images of the masculine and feminine, which have become more and more dangerously mixed in this century, be discriminated once more, so that they may come to a new synthesis in both woman and man.

It is important that we attempt to arrive at some degree of clarity about various attitudes and assumptions which are currently prevalent when people talk about woman. Those who assert that the only difference between men and women is biological, and that in every other way they are equal and have the same inborn potentialities, have disastrously missed the point. Equality of the value between individuals is an eternal truth, beyond all comparisons, whereas "superior" and "inferior" are relative terms defining abilities or degrees of consciousness. Equality of opportunity for women has indeed to be fought for, but equality of value can never be understood until we have learned to discriminate and accept *difference*. The biological difference between man and woman is never a "nothing but"; it is a fundamental difference, and it does not stop with the body but implies an equally fundamental difference of *psychic* nature. No matter how consciously we may develop the contrasexual principle within us, no matter how strong our intuition of the ultimate union between the masculine and feminine elements in each individual, yet as long as we remain in our bodies here in space and time, we are predominantly either male or female, and we forget this at our peril. Disaster awaits a woman who imitates man, but even a woman who aims at becoming half man, half woman, and imagines she is thereby achieving archetypal "androgyny" will certainly be inferior on both counts. A woman is born to be essentially and wholly a woman and the more deeply and consciously she is able to know and live the spirit, the Logos, within her, the more surely she will realize this truth. One of the most frightening characteristics of our present *Zeitgeist* is the urge to destroy difference, to reduce everything to a horrible sameness in the cause of "equality."

Whether a woman is efficient or brilliant in spheres hitherto deemed masculine, or whether she remains in a traditionally feminine role, modern woman must discriminate and relate to the image of the spirit, while at the same time maintaining her roots in her basic feminine nature—that which receives, nourishes, and gives birth on all levels of being through her awareness of the earth and her ability to bring up the water of life from under the earth. All her true creativeness springs from this.

As we look back on the extremely rapid emergence of woman in this century into the masculine world of thought and action, it is not surprising that she has fallen into increased contempt for her own values. It has surely been a necessary phase, but its effects have been devastating not only on woman herself but also on the men around her. For the animus—the unconscious masculinity in a woman—when he has taken possession of her femininity, has a terrifying power, charged as he is with the numinosity of the unconscious—and most men in their turn, when faced with this power in their women, either retreat into an inferior passive femininity, seeking to propitiate the animus power, or else react with brutal aggressive masculinity. Small wonder that women thus possessed, having lost their true roots in nature, are constantly beset by the anxious feeling of being useless, however outwardly successful. The dreams of modern women are full of this basic insecurity.

It is time then for woman to turn from this hidden contempt for the feminine values so that she may cease to identify creativity solely with the productions of thought and with achievements in the outer world. It is exceedingly hard for us to realize, in the climate of Western society, that the woman who quietly *responds* with intense interest and love to people, to ideas, and to things, is as deeply and truly creative as one who always seeks to lead, to act, to achieve. The feminine qualities of receptivity, of nurturing in silence and secrecy are (whether in man or woman) as essential to creation as their masculine opposites and in no way inferior.

But these are all rational thoughts *about* the situation. What of the images without which, as I said at the outset, no change is possible? How is a woman, when she feels the immense fascination of the power of the spirit stirring in her, to welcome it and yet remain true to her womanhood, or how is she to rediscover her femininity if she has lost it? How is a man to realize the values of the heart without losing the bright sword of his spirit in the fogs of emotion? There are no intellectual answers. Only the images by which we live can bring transformation. The future hangs on this quest for the heart of love by both sexes.

Each of us has a well of images within, which are the saving reality, and whence may be born the individual myth carrying the meaning of a life. That new images are now emerging in the tales and poetry of our time is now beyond doubt. But any truly valid "new myth" cannot be rationally invented. It must be born out of the crucible of our own struggles and suffering as we affirm our new freedom without rejecting the perennial truth of the feminine way.

ONE

The Life of the Spirit in Women *

The Spirit and the Animus

What is meant by the word *spirit?* There are a thousand answers, but the true meaning is glimpsed by us only through the kind of experience that can never be rationally explained in words. Only the images which perennially emerge from the unconscious of humankind may convey in a symbol the power of the spirit.

The most universal of all the images of the spirit is the breath, the wind—the *pneuma* in Greek, the *ruach* in Hebrew; it is that which "bloweth where it listeth and no man knoweth whence it cometh and whither it goeth." Closely related to this is the image of fire. Out of the wind came fire, the ancients believed. At Pentecost there came a rushing mighty wind and tongues of fire burned on each individual apostle. This wind, this fire of the spirit, must enter into a man or a woman before he or she can in truth be said to *create* anything at all. Thoughts and actions that remain untouched by this mystery may produce new forms in abundance, bringing good and evil in equal measure to our

* First published as Pendle Hill Pamphlet #230 © 1980 by Pendle Hill, Quaker Study Center at Wallingford, Pennsylvania, 19086.

collective life, but nothing is essentially changed in the psyche of man, whereas, whenever a breath of that wind or a spark of that fire lodges in mind or heart or body, we are immediately aware of some kind of newness of life.

If we look briefly at the various contexts in which the word *spirit* occurs, from chemistry to the Christian Trinity, we see that it is predominantly used on every level and without any moral connotation to express that which brings about a transformation. Oil is transformed into power through the spirit in petroleum; spirits of salt and spirits of ammonia burn and cleanse, purify and destroy; the spirit in alcohol lifts a man out of his ego and alters his personality before our eyes; angels or demons have always been invoked to work transformations for good or evil; the spirit that emerged at Pentecost ran like fire through the pagan world and gave birth to the new Christian era. And, greatest symbol of all, the Holy Spirit in the Godhead entered into a woman and transformed God himself into incarnate man. It is obvious from all this that the spirit basically manifests itself to Western man as an active principle, and therefore it has usually been associated with masculine creative power, though its feminine aspect has been known as Sophia, coexistent with God before creation.

Certainly it is fundamentally androgynous. But for most of us, having emerged to some degree from the original identity of archetypal opposites and being still far indeed from their conscious reunion, the paramount need is for discrimination between them. For until they are fully experienced as separate, they cannot unite in a holy marriage any more than two married people can achieve a conscious relationship until they know themselves as psychically separate. Therefore for the moment let us call the spirit *he* in accordance with our tradition.

One of the loudest complaints of the liberators of women has been that the dominance of the male in society has prevented women from proving that they are as creative as men. This is a half-truth, whereby the real truth of the matter is obscured and lost. The first essential, surely, in thinking about the transforming power of the spirit is to remember that it creates nothing in a vacuum. There has to be fuel before the fire will burn; there has to be earth as well as seed, before new life is created. The masculinity of the spirit is meaningless unless it enters into a feminine container, and ultimately no man can create anything without the equal participation of the woman without or the woman within. Even God could not transform himself into man without the free consent of Mary. In every creative act or transformation—intellectual, emotional or physical—the male and the female, the active and the passive, are of equal importance, and real liberation from the weight of the inferior status imposed on women lies not in the reiterated assertion that women must now strive to live like men, but in the affirmation, so difficult for us, of the *equal value* of the specifically feminine. Nothing demonstrates more clearly the real damage which has been done to us by the dominance of masculinity for so many centuries as the contempt for the feminine implicit in so much of the propaganda of the women's movements. It even creeps unrecognized into the work of some of the most far-seeing women writers of today. Indeed, it requires a great effort of consciousness in every individual woman to remain aware of this destructive spirit which is constantly whispering to her the collective judgment of centuries about the inferiority, the dullness, the uncreativeness of her passive feminine nature. Modern woman must therefore face the great danger of assuming that she has only to throw off the *yoke* imposed on her by men and develop her *spiritual* gifts in the spheres of activity now opened to her, in order to arrive at that far-off goal of androgynous being.

The great contribution of C. G. Jung towards the restoration of feminine values to Western man is often obscured by a misunderstanding of his concept of the *animus*. In Jung's terminology the animus is a personification of the *unconscious* masculinity in women, the anima being the parallel image of the feminine in a man. Being unconscious, it is necessarily projected [1] and often manifests itself in negative ways, and this has been interpreted entirely out of context by many of those who are devoted to the cause of liberation. Jung, they say, denies to woman any equality with man. He accuses her of producing second-hand opinions and engaging in all manner of inferior masculine activity, as though she were by nature incapable of real creativity. Nothing could be further from the truth. What Jung does affirm is that the creative power in a woman can never come to fruition if she is caught in an unconscious imitation of men or identification with the inferior masculinity in her unconscious. He defined the masculine as the ability to know one's goal and to do what is necessary to achieve it. As long as the animus remains *unconscious* in a woman, he will persuade her that she has no need to explore her hidden motives and will urge her to a blind pursuit of her conscious goals, which, of course, liberates her from the hard and undramatic task of discovering her real individual point of view. Unrecognized and undifferentiated, he will actually destroy in her the possibility of integrating her contrasexual powers. Her spirituality will thus remain a sterile thing and this negative animus will poison her attitude to her own nature. The true function of the animus is to act as an inner guide between the ego and the deep springs both of the spirit and of true feminine wisdom so that the woman may bring to birth a new consciousness of both. It is when he operates *between* her and the outer world, and she identifies with him, that he destroys her creativity. Esther Harding quoted Jung as saying in conversation that the true feminineness of the man is *not* the anima; likewise the true masculine spirit in a woman is *not* the animus, though he leads her to it. The conscious integration of her dormant spirit of clear discrimination alone can free the individual woman from the compulsive yoke of the negative animus. Without this freedom, no amount of liberation in the outer world can do more than throw her into another and more dangerous slavery.

The spiritual life is generally understood to mean the

interior awareness which leads humanity into relationship to God, the Creator. The danger of mistaking an experience of spirits for the experience of The Spirit has always been recognized by the wise. "It is not every spirit, my dear people, that you can trust; test them to see if they come from God" (Jerusalem Bible, I John 4:1). But this danger is greatly magnified in a time such as ours when every kind of experimentation is encouraged and promoted. It threatens a far greater number of people who are incapable of discrimination, and who, since they have been largely deprived of the rituals and collective symbols by which their souls were unconsciously nourished, seek everywhere to rediscover a numinous sense of meaning in life. Charismatic movements, and mystical or occult teachings of all kinds, spring up to meet the need of thousands who have lost contact with the spiritual in the deserts of materialistic rationalism. Groups come together to induce contact with what is all too easily called the holy spirit. Often there is simply an opening up of the unconscious which releases an experience of the numinous. Whether or not such an experience leads to a real glimpse of the transforming power of the spirit depends on the degree of awareness in the individual, and on the objectivity and humility with which she brings her vision to incarnation in her life on this earth. For the most part, these induced experiences are at once seized upon by that ambivalent pair—the anima and the animus—and the transformation remains on the level of the emotions or the will-to-power in the ego. People are then possessed by a hubris which heralds catastrophe.

How then are we to test the spirits? An illumination comes when we realize the extraordinary rightness of the name *holy* spirit—the spirit of the *whole*. The writer of the epistle of John, exhorting his readers to test the spirits, went on, "You can tell the spirits that come from God by this: every spirit that acknowledges that Jesus Christ has come in the flesh is from God" (Jerusalem Bible, I John 4:2). In modern psychological language this is to say that we are justified in speaking of the spirit of God only when it leads to an incarnation in us, however small, of the spirit of truth within. This is the spirit that speaks through the *daimon* of each man or woman, calling the individual to the fulfillment of his or her unique task. On the other hand, if, when the emotion of a numinous experience is spent and the darkness returns, we simply fall from exaltation to depression; or, worse, if we find ourselves so inflated by it that we at once set out to convert others, we may be sure that we are simply possessed by the *spirits* of the undifferentiated opposites in the unconscious. The true experience is always a sacrifice of the ego's one-sidedness; it is a reception of the creative seed into the vessel of the feminine, whether in man or in woman, and usually the beginning of a long nurturing, a patient waiting for the hidden birth. "Be it unto me according to thy word."

Woman and the Earth

It follows from the preceding reflections that before a woman can safely pursue her goals with the true masculine discrimination that will bring her to maturity, she must first learn to recognize and to value the nature of the principle which is dominant in her by the fact of her sex. I am not denying the obvious truth that there is a great difference in the balance of the male and female elements in each person, but, whether the difference is great or small, nature tips the scale at our conception one way or the other, and no growth or transformation is ever possible until we have accepted the facts.

In innumerable counselling situations the tragic alienation of women from their femininity becomes clear. Very often the first extremely difficult task for the modern woman is to recognize her conscious and unconscious delusions about the nature of womanhood, so that she may begin to realize the extent to which her second-hand thinking is in collusion with her repressed shadow qualities, directing her behavior and even possessing her soul. This alienation must bring with it a sense of deep guilt, since it is a betrayal of one's own birthright, and this guilt is felt in all the wrong contexts and is sometimes accompanied by a sentimental religiosity in which the spirit of Christianity is lost indeed. The neuroses which result are often the saving grace because of the suffering they bring; they are a true operation of the spirit striving to awaken the woman to her predicament.

Often such a woman will reveal at once that her concepts of what it means to be a woman are concocted from notions of frivolous, emptyheaded pleasure seekers pursuing sexual goals, plus an image of the dependent drudge condemned to sweeping floors or to a boring twenty-four-hour-a-day care of children. Half-consciously it all adds up to a choice between whoredom and slavery, though she may not define it in this way. The first she despises, the second she fears, or vice versa, and thus she is miserably caught in an interpretation of womanhood as a choice between using men or being used by them. Yet the instinct of the feminine is precisely to *use* nothing, but simply to give and to receive. This is the nature of the earth—to receive the seed and to nourish the roots—to foster growth in the dark so that it may reach up to the light.

How are women to recover their reverence for and their joy in this great archetype of which the symbols have always been the earth, the moon, the dark, and the ocean, mother of all? For thousands of years the necessity of freeing consciousness from the grip of the destructive inertia and from the devouring quality, which are the negative side of the life-giving mother, rightly gave to the emerging spirit of activity and exploration an enormous predominance; but the extremes of this worship of the bright light of the sun have produced in our time an estrangement even in women themselves from the patient nurturing and enduring qualities of the earth, from the reflected beauty of the silver light of the moon in the darkness, from the unknown in the deep sea of the unconscious and from the springs of the water of life. The way back and down to those springs and to the roots of the tree is likewise the way

on and up to the spirit of air and fire in the vaults of
heaven.

If we read the second sign of the I Ching, K'un the Receptive, which describes the Yin, the feminine principle, the
equal and opposite of Yang the Creative, we shall find
beautifully expressed there the essence of these things:

> The Earth's condition is receptive devotion.
> Perfect indeed is the sublimity of the Receptive.
> All beings owe their birth to it because it
> receives the heavenly with devotion.
> . . . Seek not works but bring to completion . . .
> To hide beauty does not mean to be inactive.
> It means only that beauty must not be displayed
> at the wrong time.[2]

The Receptive does not lead but follows, since it is like a
vessel in which the light is hidden until it can appear *at the
right time.* Thus it has no need for a willed purpose or for
the prestige of recognized achievement.

Two warnings are added—the first is against the danger
of inertia: "When there is a hoarfrost underfoot, solid ice is
not far off." The second speaks of the destructive results
when the passive value takes the lead and *opposes* the active forces of Yang. It then produces real evil if held to. It
may simply swallow up any new growth of consciousness.

If we can rediscover in ourselves the hidden beauty of
this receptive devotion; if we can learn how to be still
without inaction, how to "further life" without willed purpose, how to serve without demanding prestige, and how to
nourish without domination: then we shall be women
again out of whose earth the light may shine.

The Academic Woman

A friend confided to me the other day that she still suffered
from guilty feelings because she felt incapable of producing
original thoughts. These feelings came to her, she said,
especially at moments when she had read a book of great

creative originality to which she had felt an immediate response. She would ask herself why she was always able to follow but not initiate. Very few woman who have grown up in this century are free from this brand of guilt complex in one form or another. To those of clear mind and differentiated feeling, it may come in the manner expressed by my friend. In a great many others the guilt produces a positively compulsive desire to go to school—to acquire academic degrees—to own pieces of paper with printed evidence of achievements which will, they believe, prove at last that they are people of worth. As long as the degrees are necessary for a person's work or for a stimulus to expansion of the mind, it is well and good; but the drive often has little or no relationship either to practical necessity or to a genuine love of learning. It is found not only in those who have been deprived of opportunities for university education but frequently also in the well educated and intellectually brilliant. It is a drive far more damaging to women than to men and much more often found in them because, although a man may feel cheated of opportunities if he has not been to college, his sense of worth as a person rarely depends upon it. But the acquisition of mental and rational skills appears to innumerable modern women as the only way to escape the sense of inferiority that besets them.

A highly intelligent and able woman told me that her fear of not achieving a doctorate was driving her into a state of neurotic anxiety which was affecting her whole life. She had a good marriage, children, a teaching job which she enjoyed and did well and for which a doctorate was in no way necessary. Yet because the prestige attached to it seemed to her the only thing that could give her any real assurance of her worth, she was pouring a huge amount of her vital energy into research for her thesis. She could have explored her chosen subject without pressure and for the joy of it, once the desperate need for academic status was removed, but because of this imagined need the joy was, of course, lost. The anxiety thus generated, and the ever-growing resistance from the unconscious which made it harder and harder for her to write anything, was affecting her health and her relationships with family, colleagues and friends, and worst of all, it was progressively cutting off the springs of her sense of meaning in the unconscious. She had no time outwardly and no energy inwardly to be still and listen. Thus the earth and the water of womanhood in such a person is scorched and dried up by the destructive forces of fire and air. This may sound like an extraordinary and exaggerated state of affairs: on the contrary, it is very common among women with unusual thinking abilities.

The onset of severe neurosis in a woman of this quality of mind usually occurs, in my experience, when she is approaching the mid-point of life, and when she has already achieved considerable success in her profession. I knew one such woman who was a fine scholar and was also highly thought of as a teacher by both faculty and students. She had a good marriage and two young children; and to all who knew her superficially it would seem that the gods had indeed blessed her with every ingredient for a full and balanced life in which both her feminine eros and her masculine logos qualities could blossom. Yet when I first knew her she was suffering from neurotic symptoms so severe that her job was threatened and her children were obviously disturbed. She was subject to attacks of dizziness that would come upon her in the middle of her classes or while driving her car, and she struggled on with great courage as her fear increased. She began to explore the images in her unconscious, and she soon recognized the recurring theme through dream after dream in which she sought desperately to establish a sense of identity and meaning in her life through the prestige of mental activity acceptable to examiners or academic gatherings of men. It also became very clear that what she was really searching for was a new religious attitude to life—in short, for the inspiration of the spirit, and that this spirit had become almost wholly identified with the pseudo-masculine activity of her animus.

She had in her youth been in true and living contact with the symbolic life of the Catholic Church, and through it she had been nourished inwardly. But for modern persons with a capacity for consciousness the old unconscious nourishment is not enough. If they are not to lose contact with the living water of faith and the flame of the spirit, each one must find these things individually as well as collectively through real self-knowledge and attention to her own spontaneous imagery. If an intellectually gifted woman does not set out on this path, she is apt gradually to fall prey to the negative animus who so easily disguises himself as the true Logos. Unseen and unrecognized he takes to himself and uses as a weapon the mistrust and contempt for the feminine way, which surrounds us all. My friend had succumbed to this danger, and, although when I met her she was still trying to keep the spirit alive in herself by outer allegiance to her church, her interior life was growing more and more meaningless because of her alienation from her own truth and from the mystery of being. Very well, it may be said, if what she needs is a renewal of spirituality, let her turn to some strenuous spiritual discipline or charismatic group so that she may experience the "rushing mighty wind" or the sudden flame. Or others may recommend that she undertake some creative writing in her field which will give a sense of meaning. But these things are in themselves no cure for such a condition; neither asceticism, forced meditation, short cuts to the numinous, emotional release, nor the foredoomed attempt to create out of a sterile soil can avail unless and until she finds and experiences what it means to be a woman.

As has been said, no one, either man or woman, creates anything without the co-operation of the contra-sexual element, but when a woman of the kind I am describing tries to produce original work she goes at it, as it were, upside down. She starts from second-hand masculine thinking and is frustrated—even panic-stricken, when the feminine soil on which she is working refuses to come to life. And this situation extends into her whole life. She has then to learn to start from the receptive, the hidden, the goal-less aspect of Yin, and gradually the true light of the spirit will shine in the darkness, and the intellect too will be illumined and come to its fruition.

For a highly educated woman to learn again to trust that feminine kind of thinking, which Jung has called the natural mind, when once she has lost faith in it, is an inner quest demanding indeed the "perseverance of a mare," as the *I Ching* says. In *Memories, Dreams, Reflections* Jung described the strange irrational appearance of the feminine natural mind in his own mother, and we feel the great importance of this in his boyhood years when he found in it nourishment for his own extraordinary early awareness of the two kinds of thinking. But once lost by the instinctive woman it is only reborn through a conscious and painful sacrifice. For my friend it took the form of a decision to resign from her fine university job for an un-specified length of time—to stay at home with her children, to dig in her garden, to apply her imagination and her powers of discrimination outwardly in her cooking and housekeeping and in observing her daily reactions to her family—and inwardly by quiet attention to the images be-hind her life, which had for so long been ignored.

"What a comedown!" is the almost universal reaction to such a decision in this day and age. "Dr. So-and-so is wasting her great talents on work which any ignorant per-son can do," and so on. The encounter with this lack of understanding brings with it the crucial experience, the cross without which there is no individuation, no rebirth into a new awareness of the meaning for which one was born.

My friend faced the misunderstandings, the hostility, the loneliness, and accepted the loss of that prestige which is the life blood of the negative animus. Support from a few she had. All have need of it from at least one person at such moments, and it is always there if we have courage enough to face the vital choice. Perhaps only women who have made a similar sacrifice can fully appreciate the awful feeling of the loss of all known landmarks, the sense of failure, the fear of worthlessness, that comes to one who makes this choice.

I am not, of course, suggesting that all women with such a problem must make their sacrifice in this particular way. But in some form or other the break must be made—a defeat accepted—a loss of prestige endured, even if it is not recognized as such by others. I remember that Simone Weil wrote in one of her essays that an essential ingredient in the soul's journey through affliction was the experience of social rejection—and that whether this was suffered neurotically (to use our language) through projection, or in outer fact was not important so long as the resulting affliction was fully accepted and endured—in which case, of course, the projection is finally made conscious and can be withdrawn.

At this point it may be helpful to digress for a moment and look at the case of a man who had to go through a similar crisis—the similarities to the woman's predicament and the differences. In the case cited, the neurotic conflict was evident in the long-continued inability of this intelligent and deeply religious man to write his doctoral thesis. All his studies were done; his notes were completed, but the minute he sat down to write, a compulsive block took over and in agony of mind and heart, he sought one escape after another. He had come at last to the final year of the permissible extensions of time; his sense of inferiority was profound and he sought by sheer will and discipline to force himself to write; in his case there was a necessity to get the doctorate if he was to keep his job in the university in which he was greatly respected as man and teacher. He could not do it. For some time it had been obvious that the resistance was not in this man a mere weakness, as he had persisted in believing, but was a true protest from the unconscious. His *daimon* simply would not allow him to proceed along the royal road of a distinguished and safe academic career. He was, in fact, a priest, and his vocation was a spiritual, not an intellectual, one. But he could not pass straight from the one to the other. Suddenly he knew that the resistance was not a weakness and recognized it at last as a voice of the spirit speaking to him like Balaam's ass, standing in the way and refusing to let his master pass along a road which for him meant disaster. It had come to him not as a clear voice from on high, but from a stubborn, donkey-like, totally irrational resistance working through the instinctive wisdom of his *feminine* unconscious. He, too, made a great choice. He resigned his job in spite of the well-meaning opposition of almost all, and for two years or more he taught small children in a remote place.

So far the essentials are the same; the intellectual life has been substituted for the spiritual in both the man and the woman, as in countless others of both sexes. The immediate sacrifice was also the same—the giving up of a job which carried great prestige and security for an unknown future. The saving resistance came also from the same source—from the rejected feminine values of feeling and from the repressed natural mind which is without the goals of the conscious will. In this man's new work his energy was released from the hopeless struggle, his feeling qualities matured, and he had time and leisure to look within and search for the dominant thought in his life. He endured his spiritual conflict and found his vocation as priest which he had almost lost in those days of academic struggle. With it his authority as a man emerged, whereas before he had been in many ways still a boy. Thereupon without any effort on his part the way opened for him, and all he had sacrificed was restored to him in a priestly instead of in an intellectual context. His prestige returned, but he was no longer imprisoned in it or dominated by it. His spirit was set free to grow, nourished now by the earth of the feminine within him.

In the woman's case, however, the outcome was surprisingly different. Inwardly she made contact with her womanhood as he did with his masculine strength, but she also discovered that, unlike the man, she did indeed have a vocation to the academic life. A woman with that kind of talent is usually born to develop and to live it. His resistance came from the straightforward fact that he had mistaken his calling and rejected the feminine values, and hers was the voice of her spirit crying out to her that she would fail altogether in her true calling as teacher and thinker because she was trying to follow it at the expense of her womanhood, in imitation of men, instead of allowing it to grow out of the earth of her feminine nature.

She, then, had returned to her *earth* as best she could. At first she felt clumsy, inept, moving in an alien element. Yet she persevered through all her doubts and consented with *receptive devotion* to employ her animus on work that brought no sense of achievement, to the making of those child-like pictures and fantasies, called by Jung active imagination, which seem to the rational mind entirely pointless. Most of all, outwardly she was helped by a suddenly discovered love of gardening, of planting and tending growing things. It is not to be supposed that the animus accepted all this lying down; he produced emotional storms and worked on her sense of failure with renewed vigor. But these affects were not merely negative. They forced her to remember and to affirm her calling to academic life and her need for it. But first she had to endure the waiting and hide the light of her mind until the right time should come. She was in *the service of the King*, who is the Self, and who demands that we seek not works but completeness in our lives.

Thus, as in so many, the cause of the neurosis in both the man and the woman lay in their subjection to the collective contempt for the feminine way of *receptive devotion*.

Marie-Louise Von Franz, in her studies of the feminine in fairy tales, points out how frequently the way of the heroine involves a considerable time of withdrawal from the world, which for us means introversion, when she must go apart and endure the suffering of silent waiting for the time of her deliverance. Then comes the moment of a mature and conscious reunion with the hero, whose quest, in contrast, has involved vigorous action.

So it is within the individual. The woman had to wait for the return of her creative spirit. The time came when she felt ready to teach again. The many anxieties surrounding the work also returned to plague her, but she faced them now with far more detachment and acceptance. Then, unsought by her, came a suggestion that she apply for a position involving administration as well as teaching, and giving scope for all her exceptional qualities of mind and personality. It was time for the new light to shine. To this woman, as in the case of the man, the new opportunity came at the exact moment of readiness. The synchronicity is impressive; always it is manifest when the spirit is truly at work.

Let it not be supposed that through any of our human transformations we are freed from our conflicts. The healing of a neurosis comes not from a removal of the conflicts that were its cause, but precisely by a realization of the reality of these conflicts and by a full and free acceptance of the suffering they bring. "All opposites are of God—therefore man must bend to their burden, and in so doing he finds that God in his 'oppositeness' has taken possession of him, incarnated himself in him. He becomes a vessel filled with divine conflict." [3] That which used to be so laden with guilt and pettiness is filled with meaning.

When she returned to her calling and took up this new and exacting work, my friend had to face extreme pressures from outside and from her own insecurity, but she was now able to carry them by virtue of a fundamental change in her whole attitude to the receptive in life. She could now begin to "carry the outer world" and her own conflicts. Her reborn eros brought new warmth and acceptance into her relationships, and her teaching and work of leadership now sprang more and more from that response to meaning which *is* the creative gift of woman.

If women in work of an intellectual or administrative kind were to remember that their greatest contribution to this world of reason and logic comes from the feeling responses of their nature, much of the wreckage caused by personality clashes and neuroses could be averted. This does not mean that they are not to *think*. On the contrary, their thinking may well be of a particularly clear and incisive nature, because it springs from their own truth of feeling. Every good teacher knows that on her love for the subject she is teaching depends her ability to pass it on to others. Responding to her love with heart and mind together, she so recreates the subject that others in their turn may respond.

This brings us back to the comment about lack of original thinking in women. It is indeed easy for all to fall prey to this unconscious assumption that only original thoughts are worthy of being called creative, and so to lose sight of the truth that feminine originality lies in the capacity for unique individual *responses*, and that this is every bit as creative as the production of new ideas. This is the sure vocation of the majority of women; only the few are born to make new discoveries in the realm of ideas. Nothing can stop the genius of these few—Mme. Curie, for instance— but it is a real tragedy when so much is lost to the world by the efforts of finely endowed women to create in an imitative masculine way, instead of responding to the images either in themselves or in the work of others, thus bringing fruition to their own creative spirits.

Is this *creative resonance*, as Jung called it, an inferior thing? A woman is not truly liberated until she knows its supreme value with her whole self.

Woman in the Arts
It is an obvious fact that not only in the realm of thought but also in the arts there have been very few women of towering genius in comparison with men. We do not know what the future may bring, now that equality of opportunity is increasingly real and the weight of belief in the *proper* work of woman is lifted. There is, of course, already an enormous flowering of talent among women in every

sphere, but it may well be that for as long as we still live in
the dimensions of time and space, where differentiation
between the masculine and the feminine is the essential for
consciousness, the number of women manifesting artistic
and literary *genius* will remain small.

I hasten to add that this is not to say that the extraordinary influx of the spirit which we call genius comes more
often to men than to women. Surely there have always
been as many women as men in this rare category, but
usually we do not see the feminine genius because it does
not often come to expression in an art or science but is at
its greatest in the sphere of relationship. Even those who
are most indebted to it are sometimes quite unaware of the
unseen genius in mother or wife or friend which has
created the atmosphere wherein their own spirits have
been nourished and set free. So the *creative reasonance of
the feminine being* remains unrecognized.

It is significant that in the performing arts the
achievements of women have equalled those of men.
Names of superlatively great actresses, dancers, singers,
come quickly to mind—Mrs. Siddons, Duse, Bernhardt,
Pavlova, Jenny Lind, for example. In one branch of
literature—the art of fiction—there have also been several
women among the giants. But when we seek to name poets,
painters or composers, the contrast is obvious. There are a
number of fine women poets, but in the *supreme* category,
after naming Sappho, we pause to reflect—Emily Dickinson, Emily Brontë perhaps, and then? Almost no painters
leap into memory and interestingly enough no composers
at all, music being the most spiritual, the furthest from the
earth, of all the arts.

Acting and dancing are in their essence arts of response
and therefore peculiarly feminine. The artist becomes a
vessel for the spirit of the character he or she represents,
and this character is recreated by each great performer.
The writing of fiction likewise depends on response, on the
feeling for relationships between people and things. This
kind of response is, of course, not at all the same thing as an

instinctive reaction. On the contrary, only when the spirit of clear, discriminating intelligence fertilizes her responses does the woman's re-creation of that which she receives from another become an act of individual genius. Christmas without a conscious response to the Annunciation is unthinkable.

The stature of an artist is rarely known in his or her own time, and anyway I am not competent to make any critical judgments. It is, however, certain that the creative spirit in woman is everywhere expressing itself in the arts with great vitality and not least in the grand art of poetry. How much of this work will emerge as lastingly great we cannot yet know. Meanwhile, the openness of all true artists to the collective forces in the unconscious always carries with it specific dangers for the ego, and I believe this to be particularly so for the creative woman when she is exposed to the collective pressures of the present almost universal demand for *publicity*. It is injurious enough to any artist, but for a woman it is a threat not only to her art but to the essence of her life.

I use the word *publicity* here in its widest meaning, not in the context of literary publication. One of the major psychological diseases today is the urge to make everything public; to keep anything hidden or secret is felt to be almost a crime. Emotions are evoked and expressed in large groups; mystical or spiritual experiences are shared with as many as possible; workshops are founded in which people work publicly on the most private things; and statistics are collected with fervor so that all manifestations of the human spirit may be documented and publicized as indisputable truth. None of this is evil in itself. The urge to share creative thoughts is an essential good, and the value of group activity and of statistics is beyond question. But the extremes, sponsored by those with genuine concern for humanity as well as by the media of our society, are largely destroying the sense of mystery itself and with it the essential value of the individual *secret*, without which a man, and still more dangerously, a woman, loses contact with the soul. The individual soul cannot grow in public, for the kingdom of heaven is within, and the prayer of the spirit is in secret. "Go to your private room, and, when you have shut your door, pray to your Father who is in that secret place" (Jerusalem Bible, Matthew 6:6). As it is with prayer, so with all creative work, which is, in fact, itself a form of prayer, being an individual expression of the mystery of being. The light which is born in secret will shine out when the time is ripe and be seen perhaps by few, perhaps by many; the number is irrelevant.

Let us think of two women who were great poets and try to imagine what might have happened to them in our day. Both Emily Brontë and Emily Dickinson lived in extreme seclusion. They were withdrawn from the world; neither left home more than once or twice in the course of her life. Brontë's one novel and her few poems were among the undisputed masterpieces of the English language, but she shunned even limited publicity. Jane Austen was at great pains to perserve her anonymity. Elizabeth Jenkins says in her biography of Jane Austen, ". . . whatever the motive which led her to refuse to enter society as an authoress, she was actually obeying a profound instinct of self preservation . . . nothing would have induced her to accept a position, even in her family, in which she had to support a well-defined attitude or to be anything but the most ordinary of human beings; such a position would have been abhorrent to the conscious mind, and it would have threatened that capacity of vision that was the inspiration of her art." [4]

Dickinson's poetry remained relatively unknown until long after her death, and her genius has only recently been fully recognized. She had a normal desire for her work to be appreciated and published if possible, but solitude and introversion were as essential to her work as to Brontë's; and in their own times, though they were not free in the outward sense, their inner freedom was actually protected—by the very limitations we most abhor—from

the kind of struggle with the world which might have destroyed their spirits. Emily Dickinson wrote to her literary
mentor, Thomas Wentworth Higginson:

> I smile when you suggest that I delay "to
> publish"—that being foreign to my thought, as
> Firmament to Fin.
>   If fame belonged to me, I could not escape her—if
> she did not, the longest day would pass me on the
> chase—and the approbation of my Dog, would for-
> sake me—then. My Barefoot-Rank is better.[5]

It is not, of course, the fact of publication that kills, but
the attitude of our world towards it. How fortunate that
her literary adviser did not understand her! In an article in
The Saturday Review of Literature (April 19, 1975) Edward
Lucie–Smith has said that poets are no longer judged by
their work but by the sensational events of their lives.
Suicide is becoming to the public the exciting thing about
Sylvia Plath, Anne Sexton, and others.

Thus their poetry, he says, itself becomes interesting
only secondarily. Any true poet would despise this sort of
thing as far as his conscious attitude is concerned; but it is
a grotesque extreme arising from the universal climate of
our society, a climate in which the feminine qualities
wither and die because nothing is judged valuable unless it
is known to and approved by large numbers of people. No
one remains unaffected by this climate, but most vulner-
able of all are surely those very sensitive girls and women
in whom there lives the spirit of potential artistic creation,
and who are forced too soon into the fierce struggle for
public applause. Edward Lucie-Smith ends his article with
the thought that poets need the courage to say *no* to publi-
cists and admirers. These are every bit as threatening as
the old attitudes against which they protest with such ve-
hemence. The words of Emily Dickinson deeply heard restore the balance as they affirm the silent integrity of the
individual creative truth.

Fame of Myself, to justify,
All other Plaudit be
Superfluous—An Incense
Beyond Necessity—
Fame of Myself to lack—Although
My Name be else Supreme—
This were an Honorless
A futile Diadem—
    —*The Complete Poems of Emily Dickinson*

Art is born inevitably of conflict, and the outer life of the creative genius is often tragically disordered and imposes great suffering on those close to him or her. As Jung has suggested in discussing psychology and literature,[6] it is probably a matter of the energy which the spirit demands of one whose life is seized upon with such urgency that he must be true to his genius even if he has nothing left for other tasks and for human obligations. The one thing forbidden is the betrayal of his gift. Only the greatest of the great become complete individuals as well as supreme artists, while in this world. Shakespeare was assuredly one—Dante, Blake, and Goethe, perhaps. We are concerned here, however, with the many of lesser talents, especially the women, who, however superficially *free* their lives, are enslaved by the terrible pressure of the will to *do* which kills the creative genius of the feminine and hands it over to the negative animus and his pursuit of prestige or of the shocking and spuriously original. It may be, however, that the tragic lives and psychic suffering of such devoted women are the offering which will eventually re-awaken us to the values of the small, the secret, the hidden feminine muse which can produce a Brontë or a Dickinson. The conventions of society no longer protect such a one. The collective container of the family is lost and there can be no looking back, no retreat behind outer walls. We move forward to a new and challenging task—the discovery by each individual of the hidden vessel. Thus the woman poet may receive into the soil of her feminine earth the fire of the spirit and may know "the masculine and violent joy of pure creation." This is a line from the last stanza of the beautiful poem, "My Sister, O My Sisters" by May Sarton, in which she writes out of her great feminine wisdom of all these things. May we remember, whether we are artists or no, that retreat from the great spirit is far more likely in our day to take the form of a busy display of pseudo-masculine activity than of regression to the conventional femininity.

Every one of us, as we look back, must feel immense gratitude to those impassioned fighters whose individual *daimons* have made them spearheads of the great affirmation of freedom which has broken our collectively enforced servitude to the so-called feminine roles and is giving us equality of opportunity in every field of human endeavor. We are paying a very high price for freedom, but it cannot be evaded, and there is no remedy in a regressive renewal of the old sanctions.

Therefore, every individual woman who is capable of reflection and discrimination, and who lays claim to freedom, carries a responsibility to ask herself, "What kind of free spirit is it that breathes through me and is the dominant influence in my life?" To discover this is a task of self-knowledge which demands all the courage, honesty, and perseverance of which we are capable, and we have first to realize that real freedom from servitude comes only when one is capable of freely chosen *service*. We are freed from the *law* by which we have hitherto lived only through the choice of another binding commitment. We may do what we will only when we have learned the nature of love.

TWO

Goddess of the Dawn

Easter is a word most of us have used all of our lives, yet I suspect few of us have thought about its derivation. As far as I know, in all languages except the Germanic, the name of the feast of the Resurrection is derived from the Hebrew word *pesach*, the Passover. The root of the German word for Easter, *Ostern*, is the ancient Aryan word for both east and dawn. It is thought that *Ostern* became *Easter* because the name of the dawn-goddess was Eostre. (Eos is the goddess of the dawn in Greek; Aurora is the goddess in Latin.) In southern Europe Christianity spread slowly, absorbing old beliefs. It was an alien religion, however, for the Germanic peoples, so for them the greatest feast of the new faith became easily associated with their own great goddess who nurtured the light of the sun as he rose from the darkness of the night.

It seems to me that in our time, this image of the goddess bringing to birth the resurrected sun—or Son—out of the womb of darkness, out of the burial cave in the earth, carries a numinous power. For there can be no doubt that if civilized humankind is to survive the dangers of this century of transition, when all the familiar landmarks are disappearing and the collective structures that used to protect us are crumbling, we must turn to the *goddess*, to the long-despised values of the feminine, to the feeling heart and the contemplative mind. Perhaps then our culture may see the rising of a new day.

We live in a dying era. The collapse of the standards in which Christians have believed for so many centuries is obvious when we look at the terrifying spread of violence, dishonesty and greed. These things are no longer simply the inevitable rebellions against a collective ethic, but are undermining the ethic itself, destroying from below all those values of love, courtesy, responsibility and creative imagination that civilized humankind has brought to consciousness through the Christian faith. It is easy for us to put all this aside and take refuge in the perfectly sound attitude that the only valid contribution we can make to our time is to attend to our own shadow sides—to the death of old personal attitudes and the suffering of the day-to-day tension of the opposites. But while the majority of men and women need, above all things, to learn this truth, yet it is also possible to take refuge in it. We need to reflect deeply on how much we are conditioned by the *Zeitgeist* of our era, and we may then realize the great importance of the infinitesimal and yet crucial influence which goes out from each of us via the unconscious to nourish or to undermine the *pistis*, or unshakeable trust, without which there can be no Easter for our world.

The promise of the dawn is already visible in the yearning of so many people for the restoration of meaning to their lives, a meaning which the collapse of the medieval world view has taken from them. If enough individuals consciously attend and watch (as in Carl Jung's story of the Pueblo Indians) in those magical moments when both dark and light are present together in the twilight, then indeed the sun will rise on a new era. The Pueblos believed that the actual physical sun would never rise again—for them or for the white man—if they were not *there* in the dawn to greet it. Of course we know better, but the perennial *mythological truth* of their belief has been thrown out together with the withdrawal of the projection onto the material sun. Thus the inevitable death of primitive cultures has been, until recently, an extinction, instead of a transformation through resurrection, into a mythology

uniting scientific and psychological truth. Indeed, one of
the signs of the dawn we now glimpse is the resurrection at
last of the values of primitive wisdom as a result of the
work of Carl Jung and of many other individuals.

The same issues may be seen in the present overthrow of
Christian moral imperatives. Will they become extinct,
and with them our whole civilization, to be replaced by
catastrophic regression to instinctual power and greed? Or
will our old extraverted attitude to these imperatives die
through the suffering of crucifixion in the psyche of individuals? Such a crucifixion may bring a resurrection,
through the birth of a new attitude, to the unchanging values underlying the old moral imperatives. Crucifixion in
this sense is the nailing to the cross of the opposites in the
psyche and the total acceptance of the tension between
them. The values themselves remain the same, just as
Christ's body was the same after his death; yet they are
transformed into a new dimension of radiant life and
meaning, both individual and cosmic.

In his address to the Guild of Pastoral Psychology in
London in 1939, Jung said: "Christ carried out his
hypothesis to the bitter end . . . if anyone lives his [own]
hypothesis to the bitter end [and pays for it by his death
perhaps] he knows that Christ is his brother . . . I do not
care for a historic future at all, not at all. I am not concerned with it . . . My history is only the history of those
individuals who are going to fulfill their hypotheses. That
is the whole problem, that is the problem of the true Pueblo: that I do today everything that is necessary so that my
Father can rise over the horizon." [1]

Jung's statement may be misleading, for one cannot read
his works without realizing his intense concern with the
history of humankind. What Jung plainly means here is
that the usual kind of intellectual concern with historical
events is of no interest to him for it leaves out the very
thing that determines historical change—the inner life of
countless individuals. He is most deeply concerned with
the world around him in just the same way as were the

Pueblos. They *knew* that the world itself and all its peoples would remain in darkness forever if they were not there in the dawn to ensure the rising of the sun by their hope and their worship. It is scientific nonsense but a profound and unchanging inner truth.

Jung's use of the word *hypothesis* is interesting. The Oxford English Dictionary defines *hypothesis* as "a supposition made as basis for reasoning without assuming its truth." Jung means, then, that when an individual commits himself to the ruthless honesty which will lead to that which he perceives as his unique way in life, there can nevertheless be no certainty of absolute truth. Surely the meaning of the cry from the Cross, "My God, my God, why hast thou forsaken me?" is that even Christ at the bitter end had to experience a moment of recognition that the whole hypothesis of his life's work *might* have been a mistake, and, accepting this, go on to the *consummatum est*. "It is complete," and so "Into thy hand I commit my spirit."

Commitment to our unique way in life, then, is our task today and every day. It is not to be undertaken for our self-improvement, nor for the salvation of the world or society, but simply because we can do no other if we are to be true to the individual *hypothesis* of our lives. The whole meaning of Christ's message to the world is the "apotheosis of individuality," as Jung has called it. It is the theme of many dreams and of most of the great stories of the world in which the life or death of innumerable people, of nations, of the world itself, depends on a single choice by a single individual who is true or false to himself. "Does [modern man] know that he is on the point of losing the life-preserving myth of the inner man which Christianity has treasured up for him? Does he realize what lies in store should this catastrophe ever befall him? ... And finally, does the individual know that *he* is the makeweight that tips the scales?" [2]

All the ancient mysteries were concerned with a symbolic death and resurrection, through which the initiate became one with the god. The thing that differentiates the

Christian mystery from the others is that instead of being a symbolic rite alone, in which the inner truth was experienced in the unconscious, it was revealed as an incarnate experience lived consciously by a single person at a specific moment in historical time. It was also declared to be a mystery not reserved for the very few, but inherent in the psyche of every individual. Anyone who would pay the price, who would face the "crucifixion" of the opposites in whatever form they were presented to him in his own ordinary human life, could experience the death of his old ego-centered attitudes and the resurrection into a new life both in this world and in the beyond, a life in which desire is transmuted into love.

It was the centrality of love in the Christian revelation that initiated the powerful surge of civilizing creative energy at the dawning of the new age; and the second half of the 2000-year period was to bring the immense expansion of knowledge and technological power which continues today at an ever-accelerating rate. The pursuit of knowledge, however, gradually became so one-sided that the feminine feeling values of love degenerated into mere lip service and in recent years have been openly rejected and despised. Love is a word that cannot now be used without precise qualifications, since it has been debased to cover such substitutes as lust, "togetherness," mass ecstasies, and superficial good works.

The author of *The Cloud of Unknowing*, writing in the 14th century, defined the essence of the Christian revelation thus: "Rational creatures, such as men and angels, possess two principal faculties: a knowing power and a loving power. No one can fully comprehend the uncreated God with his knowledge, but *each one*, in a different way, can grasp him fully by love. Truly this is the unending miracle of love: that *one loving person* through his love, can embrace God, whose being fills and transcends the entire creation." [3]

Every man or woman, no matter how simple, can approach individuation—the living of his meaning as an individual being—if he or she will learn the nature of love. The great passage on love at the end of *Memories, Dreams, Reflections* [4] is Jung's own definition of this truth. The love of another human being—provided always that it is a *true* love—is indeed a direct way to wholeness. But a true love costs "no less than everything" and sooner or later, within and without, includes the experience of loss, a passing through death to resurrected vision—as in Dante's *Divine Comedy*.

Thus in these last years of the Christian era, if we are not to be devoured by the monstrous inflation of the "knowing power" at the expense of the "loving power" and suffer the catastrophe of which Jung spoke, then enough individuals must dare to face, not the extinction of the eternal Christian values of love, but the exceedingly painful death of our most cherished attitudes towards them. After pointing out that our conceptions of the Christian symbol have failed utterly to heal the terrible split in the western world, Jung wrote:

> This is not to say that Christianity is finished. I am, on the contrary, convinced that it is not Christianity, but our conception and interpretation of it, that has become antiquated in face of the present world situation. The Christian symbol is a living thing that carries in itself the seeds of further development . . . it depends only on us, whether we can make up our minds to meditate again and more thoroughly on the Christian premises. This requires a very different attitude towards the individual, towards the microcosm of the Self, from the one we have adopted hitherto.[5]

The individual alone is the "carrier of life." The death with which we are faced is the death of the dependence and ultimate submergence of the individual in the group—any kind of group, from the great institutions to the smallest gathering. This is not to say that there is no place for groups any more, for churches and great institutions, but it does mean the death of old dogma*tisms*. It does not mean the death of dogma itself, which in its deepest meaning is a symbolic language showing forth the archetypal truths of the psyche, but the death of the claims to impose it in unchanging literal interpretations. Then there may come indeed a resurrection into a transformed symbolic life within the members of such groups who are striving to meet together for worship or action as free individuals.

The fundamental demand for individual freedom arising from the unconscious in our time is being met on all sides by the horrors of individual*ism* and the throwing off of all restraints and responsibilities. This in its turn creates panic and produces the equally dangerous frantic patching up of the old attitudes and imposed beliefs through the reestablishment of groups and institutions on a reformed but not basically regenerated basis. The evasions of the way to greater consciousness are legion. Among them may be such things as the well-meant attempts to awaken "spiritual experiences" through suggestion in groups; admirable social welfare movements based on theories in which progress is identified with collective rather than individual change; "loving" communities in which relationships are lost in an unconcious merging; and all the quick panaceas for our psychic and physical ills that have become so familiar. All these may, with the best intentions, turn easily to substitutes for the lonely way. Everyone needs the support of others in varying degrees, and sharing between individuals and in groups is essential, but *submergence* in a group brings neither real support nor any true exchange or relatedness.

It is easy to lose hope when we look clearly at the immensely powerful forces that are pushing us into one or the other of these dangers of individualism or of group thinking and feeling; but let us continually remember the dreams, the stories, the myths, which declare the unshakeable truth that the single individual—you or I—may be the "makeweight that tips the scales."

In our psychological age we can approach the images

with a new objectivity. The myths either die and then descend into superstition, or they grow and expand into a deeper life. Through these images, I believe that we can come most directly to a connectedness with the time in which we live. We stand, as did the Pueblos, in the dawn light of a new era.

For thousands of years the symbolic imagery of astrology has put men and women in touch with the archetypal meaning behind human life. Like all images through which people have experienced the numinous, those of astrology have to do with "the acausal orderedness of the universe," to use Jung's phrase. The language of astrology expresses the fundamental synchronicity in the universe.

The age of Aries ended around 7 B.C. The ram is the sacrificial animal, and symbolically we think of Abraham's sacrifice of the ram instead of his son as a point of great transition from complete identification with the unconscious (which involved the necessity of sacrificing human beings to expiate guilt) to the beginnings of a symbolic life in which the sacrifice could be projected onto an animal which "gave itself" to save the conscious man. The same theme is evident in the story of the Passover. The chosen people were passed over when the angel of the Lord came to take the first-born of those who had not awakened to the era of Aries. The Israelites dedicated their eldest sons to God and were fed by the sacrificed ram. Thus they pledged themselves to the "making holy" of their blind instinctive urges and could set forth on the long road to the new land, to which they were guided by the *law* of Moses.

Christ's death was the new Passover, the revelation of the meaning of the era to come. Human beings could no longer project their "sacrifice" onto the animal creation and confine their efforts to the control of instincts through law. This had been a necessity for the growth of consciousness; but the sacrifice of the Lamb of God became a symbol of the conscious offering possible for individual human beings—the offering of one's whole self, instinctive, affective, reasoning, even the divine nucleus of one's being.

Eventually men and women could learn to offer themselves and to become "brothers of Christ" by living their own hypotheses to the bitter end. "I live, yet not I, but Christ liveth in me," said St. Paul. The ego-centered personality had to be transformed and to become conscious of the life of the Self—a sacrifice which could only be accomplished through the power of love.

During the age of Aries, as I have said, the outer law was that which guided men and women so that the beginnings of conscious life were protected. In the new age of the fishes, the values of law were not to be extinguished but fulfilled in love. Love, however, only becomes the fulfilling of the law when a man or woman is mature enough to take up responsibility for free individual choice.

Jung wrote in *Aion:* "When the spring point moved into the constellation of the fishes there came an age in which the 'fish' was used as a name for the God who became a man, who was born as a fish and sacrificed as a ram, who had fishermen for disciples and wanted to make them fishers of men, who fed the multitude with miraculously multiplying fishes, who was himself eaten as a fish, the 'holier food,' and whose followers were little fishes." [6]

He died then as a ram or lamb and was resurrected as the fish whose flesh was to be the "holy food" throughout the 2000 years of our era. The fish, the wisdom from the waters of the unconscious, was for the first time to become the food consciously eaten not only by initiates, but by ordinary men and women. It was indeed a dawn.

After the resurrection came the most beautiful image of the opening age of the fishes—the breakfast in the early morning beside the sea of Galilee, when the disciples, fishing in the deep, saw Jesus on the shore cooking fish for them on the fire that he had built. Under the new sun they broke their fast with the food from the depths of the feminine unconscious, which they, through their awakened love, were to pass on to others. As they sat there Christ said to Peter, "Dost thou love me? Feed my sheep." For a long time to come the multitude would remain "sheep" to be fed by those who had experienced the meaning of the incarnate Christ, and also by the symbols and dogmas of the church which rose on the "rock" of the archetypal fisherman and became the great guardian of the mysteries. Through her rituals and laws she protected the "sheep" from the more terrifying implications of Christ's "apotheosis of individuality," which few could face during the age which in our time is drawing to its close.

It was inevitable, perhaps, that the new food of love rising out of the unconscious should become exclusive—as do all collectively propagated creeds—and that passionate love of the good should lead to rejection of evil instead of confrontation, and thus to moralistic repression and the attempt to eliminate the values of the natural life. This process was intensified in the Protestant churches. The Reformation was another example of the blindness whereby men and women affirm a great new movement of consciousness but attempt to extinguish the old values instead of seeking their transformation. The rigidity of the extreme dogmatism of the Roman church at that time then became in both divisions of Christianity a far more damaging rigidity of moral condemnation, and with this there came a death of the symbolic life.

Jung has used astrological symbolism to illustrate what has happened. In the sign of Pisces there are two fishes swimming in opposite directions—the Christ and the anti-Christ, his dark brother. The nature of true love is not exclusive. We cannot love and feed on the bright fish and refuse to recognize the validity of its opposite. "Love your enemies" did not mean the kind of emotional whitewashing it has so often become. It involves a stern and clear-eyed recognition of evil as it is; the courage to confront and to fight it to the death, if necessary, on one level; but at the same time a compassionate acceptance of its manifestations in oneself or in others. For the dark fish is also necessary food—equally "holy food" indeed. If we do not swallow and digest it individually, we shall inevitably be devoured by it collectively.

We are passing out of the age of the fishes; they have been drawn up out of the water, but increasingly they have been left to dry up on the shore, despised by men and women who turn to richer and more exciting foods to satisfy their hungers. Nevertheless, if we will contemplate the stars within us, we shall see, rising ahead, the image of Aquarius, the water carrier, who stands in the heavens pouring water from a never-failing jar down into the mouth of the stranded fish below him. There can be no better picture of the resurrection for which we wait. The fish is restored to life by a whole man, image of the "apotheosis of individuality," who holds consciously in the feminine vessel the living water of the depths. Moreover, in some of the ancient zodiacs the water carrier is actually shown as a woman.

The three constellations nearest to and closely associated with each zodiacal sign are called "decans." The Aquarian decans are the Southern Fish, the Winged Horse (Pegasus), and the Swan. The fish is in the unconscious; the horse is on this earth. (Pegasus was called the "horse of the gushing fountain," for when he struck the earth on Mt. Helicon with his hoof, the fountain of the muses broke forth. Therefore he is the bringer of imaginative vision to the earth.) And the beautiful swan is said to circle and mount the Milky Way into the heavens. Thus we have yet another quaternity—the man with his fire of consciousness; the fish from the feminine depths; the horse ranging the earth; and the bird of the spirit flying in the heavens. And the quintessential ruler of all is the individualized man in the image of Uranus.

Surely, then, as the spring point enters this quaternity, we may look to a new Easter—a resurrection which we may well feel to be the long expected second coming of Christ in what Jung calls the continuing incarnation in the individual woman or man. Jung always affirmed that the way of individuation was impossible for anyone without all the Christian virtues. In *Aion* he wrote that the end of the Christian era of the fishes does not mean the extinction of the profound historical significance of Christ. Rather, it means the resurrection into a new dimension of the unique and the universal simultaneously. In his Introduction to his translation of *The Cloud of Unknowing*, William Johnston quotes Teilhard de Chardin:

> We can consider Christ in his historical existence or in his risen existence. In either case it is, of course, the same Jesus but the mode of existence is quite different . . . the risen Christ contains in himself all the experience of his historical existence in a transformed way, as he indicated by showing his wounds to his disciples . . . As for the way of talking about the Christ who lives in our midst today, Teilhard de Chardin speaks of "the cosmic Christ" who is co-extensive with the universe. By death the body is universalized, entering into a new dimension, a new relationship with matter. It is in this dimension that the risen Christ is present to us.[7]

So may we stand in the dark and contemplate the goddess of the dawn who brings forth the resurrected sun. In our individual lives it means that we stand continually ready to accept the death of an old attitude, the loss of an object of love or veneration, the end of a projection that has lost its numinosity or its relevance to the present. Such things may be replaced by rationalizations, in which case the dead value inevitably becomes a ghost, haunting us from the unconscious. Even weaknesses and sins from which we have emerged with moral effort may very easily return disguised in an even more unconscious form if we do not seek the "resurrection" of the value behind the urge from which they sprang. To give one example, an alcoholic finding through devotion and discipline his freedom from that particular craving may easily feed the deep-seated longing for release from conflict, which lies below his drinking, through some other often unrecognized and outwardly respectable escape route, if he does not recognize and nourish that most essential longing of his spirit for the freedom of the risen Self.

Everything that is unconscious is projected by the psyche either into the environment or into symbols whereby the inexpressible meeting point of eternity and time may be experienced, if only for brief moments.

With our beginnings of objective psychological awareness, we may now realize that the "co-inherence" of the entire universe in its smallest manifestations is no magical belief but an indisputable inner truth. Astrology, released from cause and effect and experienced in the realm of synchronicity, is simply a language of images expressing this co-inherence. As the spring point, the resurrection point, passes from Pisces towards Aquarius, the fundamental truths and values of the Christian era, though dying in their old forms, are approaching a possible transformation into a new, as yet unknown, unity of the knowing power and the loving power—a unity which may include the life of the body itself. New levels of consciousness are emerging. The mystics have hitherto spoken of these levels, but now they are also being affirmed by quantum physics, the *hierosgamos* of matter and spirit, the realization of the *unus mundus*. It is an exciting experience to enter somewhat into imaginative contact with the profound symbolism of Pisces and of Aquarius, of the fishes and of the new whole person.

THREE

Goddess of the Hearth

Laurens Van der Post tells how he overheard a student at the Jungian Institute in Zurich saying to another student, "What is fire?" The reply was, "It is energy." "And I thought," continues Van der Post, "dear Heaven, can we be as intellectual as all that? Surely fire is light in the dark, it is warmth against cold, it is security against the beast and the things that prowl by night. People no longer see the sun as a great source of light but as gases and sunspots. The great sun-within-themselves, their interaction between what goes on in the universe and themselves, is cut off . . . Fire is just energy to us." [1]

When great symbols lose their content and their meaning for us, we are in danger of losing our souls. "This narrow, rational awareness that we have developed," says Van der Post, "has cut us off from the image-making thing in us." So great is the pressure from the collective values of our time, however, that even for those of us who recognize this truth, there is need to struggle every day so that we may avoid falling into a subtle devaluation of all our efforts towards image-making. "What's the point?" says the voice of anima or animus; "Contemplating images is a waste of time. It changes nothing." On one level that is true; it changes nothing, for it opens the door to that which is eternal, bringing all the changing phenomena of our individual lives into relationship with the unchanging whole.

But on the level of our limited consciousness, it is the only thing that changes *anything*. In particular, the contemplation of the symbol of fire, the experience in some measure of its infinity of meaning, is that which can establish the "interaction between ourselves and the universe," the rising of the "great sun within." For fire is the agent of transformation, and without it human beings would not have begun to emerge from the unconsciousness of the animal world.

For primitive man fire meant the living presence of the sun, the descent of the supreme spirit to earth, and with it came the capacity for conscious creation or destruction. Fire itself is forever the same in its essential nature, but it cannot burn at all here on earth without fuel, and it is the nature of the fuel with which a person feeds the fire, whether exterior or interior, which determines whether it will create or destroy. How exciting a thing it is when we see in imagination the first little flames kindled by the rubbing of sticks in the primeval forest! How exciting it is to remember at the same time the fire of the Spirit striking into the heart and womb of the mother of God, or the flames from above flickering on the heads of the apostles at Pentecost, and to *realize* that the great universal symbol of fire carries the same meaning at every level of consciousness! The fire descends to meet the fuel of earth and flames upward again towards its source.

The fire may kindle the wood of the hearth fire, or it may rage uncontrolled through the forest or the house; it may light the gentle wick of the candle or the tiny fuse which explodes a bomb; it may evoke the life-giving blaze of imagination, the warmth of tenderness and love, or the murderous emotions of anger and hate and lust. "The only hope or else despair lies in the *choice* of pyre or pyre,"[2] wrote T. S. Eliot.

It is the crucial matter of the choice of fuel that is the subject of the I Ching hexagram #30,[3] which is the doubled trigram meaning *Fire*. It is called "The Clinging," directing attention to the fact that fire must cling to something in order to burn at all. The words of the Judgment are somewhat of a shock. "The Clinging. Perseverance furthers. It brings success. Care of the cow brings good fortune." The image of the cow is so remote from either fuel or fire, it seems, that we are bewildered. A footnote in the Baynes-Wilhelm translation points out that in the Parsee religion the worship of fire is also associated with the cow, so that it is not a purely Chinese image.

If we look a little deeper, however, we begin to see how true it is that the moment we cease to "care for the cow," the fire either goes out or rages out of control to our destruction. Ahura Mazda, god of light and wisdom in Zoroastrianism, was nourished on the milk of the cow when he came to earth. Only the particular essence of the feminine principle symbolized by the cow can maintain the steady flame of the inner light. For the cow means something more specific than simple motherhood. *She stands in our imagination as an image of the slow, patient chewing of the cud which turns the grass of the earth into human food.* Receiving the seed of the fiery bull, she conceives, but the milk which she produces for her young may also, if consciously drawn upon, provide nourishment not only for human beings, but even for the god incarnate himself. The cow is the *passive, feminine heat of unremitting attention* without which there can be no transformation by fire. The alchemist mixing his raw materials with superlative skill in his retort could have achieved nothing if he had not tended the fire underneath it day and night, so that it might not burn too high or too low. So also must the cook watch in her kitchen, the smith in his smithy, and, most earnestly of all, every person who seeks to transform the raw material of his or her life *into the gold of consciousness.* For if the fire goes out or burns too fiercely, it is very likely that he must begin all over again. It is only if we will drink daily of the milk of the "cow" within us that we can find strength for this. One word for this inner care of the cow is *rumination,* which is derived directly from the chewing of the cud.

There is no mention at all in the hexagram of the fiery

bull. The message of the *I Ching* is to the "superior man," that is to say, in our language, to the conscious person—the person who has already recognized that the bull must be sacrificed. For the fire of which the hexagram speaks is the inner light, the great sun-within-ourselves, of which we can only be fully aware when the wild instinctive fire of the bull has been experienced, accepted, and transformed.

The bull appears again and again in antiquity as the sacrificial animal, for example in the Mithraic mysteries and in the original symbolism of the bullfight. The cow is not sacrificed, for her milk is necessary to the god, and she is therefore already sacred.

In the ox-herding pictures and poems of Zen, we see the wild bull gradually turning from black to white. First the herdsman must find the black bull; then he uses whip and lash, then a rope; then he is able to ride peacefully without bridle; at last the bull is free to roam harmlessly where he will—and now he is wholly white. The fire of indiscriminate emotion is fire from heaven like any other, burning to fulfill its nature through union with the fuel, the object of desire, but burning itself out without meaning, until through discipline, conscious watching, and acceptance, the change of fuel brings transformation and freedom. The bull is no longer black, unconscious affect; he is white, creative fire.

It is at this point that the *I Ching* warns us of danger, for the taming of the bull *may* be mere repression by a superficial, highly developed ego-consciousness. If the clarity which we have achieved turns to intellect uprooted from life and we forget the cow—if indeed we neglect the cow at any point along the way—then the fire "flames up, dies down, is thrown away," in the words of line 4. The commentary adds, "Clarity of mind has the same relation to life as fire has to wood. Fire clings to wood but also consumes it. Clarity of mind is rooted in life but can also consume it." This wisdom comes to us over 3000 years and is more urgently applicable today than ever before, for we are in danger indeed of a final flaming up, a dying, a throwing away of human life on earth precisely because of our neglect of the *cow*. Clarity of mind has become identical with intellect; because we so quickly forget or regard as *unimportant the constant chewing of the green grass of the earth*, the daily inner rumination which is the drawing of the milk of simple human kindness, the nourishment of the quiet heart.

Thus the whole course of a person's life depends on the nature of the fuel which day by day he or she feeds to the fire of being, either consciously or unconsciously. "We only live, only suspire, consumed by either fire or fire,"[4] said T. S. Eliot. When the fuel is provided by an ego dominated by unconscious desire, the fire will be a straw fire, flaring up in emotional reactions, positive or negative, power drives, or intellectual ambitions, transforming nothing. Line 3 of the hexagram refers to this. "In the light of the setting sun men either beat the pot and sing or loudly bewail the approach of old age." Not only in the matter of old age do we do this. When we burn in this way, swinging from one opposite to the other, the cow is starving, forgotten, neglected, and slowly we are consumed, become meaningless, are "thrown away."

This is one of Eliot's two fires. What of the other? The spark of the creative imagination, the objective warmth of the heart, the flames of conscious suffering, and the white fire of the Spirit—all these will burn only if we will care for the cow. Cow's milk, cow's urine, and cow's dung all partake of the holiness of the cow in India. In glaring contrast to this, there is contempt in the West for this image. To call a woman a cow is an insult. Yet even here our unconscious knows better and it has thrown up into speech the exclamation "Holy Cow." I heard someone exclaim recently, "Holy cow! How the walls of Jericho have come tumbling down!" How right the strange juxtaposition of images was! Only after the long hard times of accepting and quietly chewing the cud of facts, of maintaining patience, in the face of no visible results, does the trumpet sound and down come the walls of Jericho. The inner fire is lit, but it will burn with a steady light only so long as we feed it daily with the necessary fuel. In the story of Moses' life all this is very clear. The fire blazed up in his generous emotion of pity for the man beaten by the overseer; he fed it with an angry act, and it burned itself out in the destruction of the overseer's life. But Moses had learned the lesson. He went into the wilderness and through the long years of exile, *the quiet tending of the flocks*, the finding of his bride, his feeling nature, he took care of the cow within. He was nourished by the "milk" of his patient waiting, and, when the time was ripe, the fire blazed up again; and out of the bush which burned and was *not* destroyed (for even the fire which does *not* consume must have fuel) he heard the voice of God. So the fire of his spirit was kindled and all through his long life of devotion it burned steadily on the fuel of his accepted responsibility and his endurance, his unremitting care for his people. The fierce heat burned out in him all his ego-concern; it kept alive the pillar of fire by night; it turned aside the wrath of God. Only once did he fall and feed it with personal anger, identifying with the fire itself when he struck the rock, oblivious for that brief moment of the patient "cow" whose milk was his sustenance through those long years. This milk alone it is which ensures the burning which does not destroy and from which the voice of God speaks to a man or a woman.

The artist must similarly feed the *burning fire of his vocation*. The fuel of his art, the hard discipline and often agonizing work of making his vision incarnate, will soon be abandoned and the fire burn itself out if he will not "care for the cow," will not endure the dry periods when the flame of imagination seems totally extinct, will not learn the slow tempo of the cow, while in the passive feminine womb of the unconscious the seed matures. Blake is a shining example of an artist whose inner fire burned with such terrifying power that it threatened to consume him utterly and destroy his sanity. He was saved by his "care of the cow." He married a woman with whom, it seems, he was not passionately in love, but with her he was able to build a home rooted in the simple values of earth, and in it was lit the hearth *fire of quiet day-by-day devotion.* Thus he was nourished on the milk of human warmth and relatedness, and the fire was contained so that he could give enduring form to his burning visions.

By long years of caring for the cow the brightness is *perpetuated*, and in men like Blake, the great sun-within-themselves shines out into life and back from the four quarters of the world to the center of their being. They have achieved "interaction between themselves and the universe."

The *I Ching* speaks of the great man, but all of us, however small we may feel, can become aware to some degree of this brightness and can perpetuate this awareness. Our danger is more often that the fire of imagination will go out for lack of fuel than that it will blaze up and destroy us. All have somewhere buried away the capacity for image-making, and the little spark can be nursed into a blaze only if we will care for our cow. She must be milked without fail, morning and evening, or she will sicken and die. We must draw the milk and drink it; otherwise the patience which seeks out the right twigs to feed the flames will soon peter out, and under our conscious apathy, we will be feeding the destructive fires below. A cow cannot wait very long to be relieved of her milk. A farmer cannot say, "I am too busy today," or, "I don't feel like it." But to modern men and women, these two phrases are a constant justification of his neglect of the cow.

The feeding of the hearth fire is, of course, the special concern of woman. We think of the hearth as the center of the feeling life of the family and its *quality depends upon the mother*—the mother in each of us whether we have physical children or no. Therefore it is startling at first when we remember that the Goddess of the Hearth in ancient Greece was Hestia, a virgin. Her Roman name was Vesta and the sacred hearth fire of the city was tended by the Vestal Virgins. This has a profound meaning for us. The central warmth of a home will be a matter of fleeting emotions—blazing up, going out, overheating or underheating—unless the woman who tends the hearth fire is in touch with her *virginity;* unless she nourishes the fundamental feeling values from that part of perself which is "virgin" in the ancient sense of the word, for it originally meant *"she who is one-in-herself."* Philo of Alexandria said that when a virgin lay with a man she became a woman, but when God began to have intercourse with the soul, she who was woman became virgin again.

To the extent, then, that a woman has found herself as separate, one-in-herself, has freed her emotional life from possession and possessiveness, to this degree only can she bring unity to the family around the hearth. Even if she lives physically alone, the image holds. As she grows to this maturity of feeling she will tend the hearth fire day and night, as the Vestal Virgins tended the hearth fire of the city. The virginity of the Mother of God, which is so thin a concept when confined to the physical plane, takes on its full and overwhelmingly beautiful meaning when we begin to be aware of these things in our ordinary daily lives. *No woman has found a true relationship with a man or the real meaning of motherhood until she has also to some degree found herself consciously as virgin—one-in-herself.* We do well to remember at this point the symbol of the holy prostitute in the ancient mysteries of woman, for the conventional meaning of virginity as a refusal of sexual experience so easily creeps back into our thinking. The woman's giving of her body to "the stranger" in the temple brings home to us the strange paradoxical truth that a woman cannot become "virgin" in the conscious sense unless she is *capable* of a total giving of herself, body as well as soul. She must burn in the fires of instinct, and then be *willing* to give herself totally to "the stranger," that is, where her emotions are not involved, or perhaps, as Esther Harding has said, to do the hardest thing of all for the feminine psyche, to allow herself to love with her whole being someone from whom she knows she can expect no return, no fruition.

The experience of virginity is not a cold thing. It may be

felt with a burning intensity at moments when the body is on fire with unfulfilled desire, provided one is consciously aware that this desire will, if we endure and contain it, consume the demands of our concupiscence, while proclaiming the beauty of instinct and its validity. An experience of this nature has a kind of cleanness and purity which is the essence of real virginity. These things she can only do when she begins to live the symbolic life—to enter the temple and become a prostitute therein. From it she emerges a virgin and the hearth fire will burn wherever she may be and many will be warmed and strengthened thereby.

None of this, however, can possibly come about in her if she neglects her essential feminine cow-likeness. She must *produce* milk, not only drink it. Through all her experiences, from virgin to woman to virgin again, she must constantly *digest the green grass of her earthly experience* and give the milk of her feminine warmth to all who will draw it, not thrusting it at people, but simply letting it down at the touch of a milker's fingers.

Finally the fires of desire, of imagination, of the heart, all the lesser fires of our experience, bring us to the purging fire of sacrifice. Jung has said that in some traditions the cross is a symbol of fire, and that this may be due to the association with the rubbing of two sticks to produce fire. Primitives thought of these as masculine and feminine. They meet, and the rubbing, the friction between them, brings the fire of life to earth. The Christian cross is, of course, the great symbol of the fire of suffering. "Whosoever is near to me is near to the fire," is an apocryphal saying of Christ. There comes a time when it is no longer a question of tending fires, of finding fuel, but of becoming ourselves the fuel, walking open-eyed into the flames.

In our dreams we find images of all the different kinds of fuel which determine the nature of the fire in our lives, the direction of all our psychic energy. Dreams of fires burning and destroying indiscriminately will tell us of the raging of unacknowledged emotions in the unconscious; dreams of the hearth fires lit in the wrong places or of furnaces in the basement, either with flames leaking out or stone cold, warn us to look to the "virginity" of our feelings; dreams of fire cooking food speak of the alchemical transforming process at work and candles burning steadily awaken quiet devotion. We may see a light blazing in darkness, illuminating, bringing consciousness, or a fire on which burns a symbol of some old attitude to be sacrificed. Occasionally there comes a great dream of the fire into which we must voluntarily enter and give ourselves up.

Through "care of the cow" all these images may be "perpetuated" and experienced as daily reality. Then indeed the "great-sun-within" begins to rise and to illuminate the four quarters of the world, the four-fold wholeness of the individual person. So finally we may come to know "the condition of complete simplicity" of which T. S. Eliot speaks in *The Four Quartets* where "the fire and the rose are one." [5]

FOUR

Mother and Daughter Mysteries

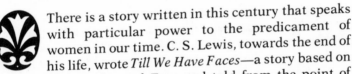 There is a story written in this century that speaks with particular power to the predicament of women in our time. C. S. Lewis, towards the end of his life, wrote *Till We Have Faces*—a story based on the myth of Psyche and Eros and told from the point of view of one of the ugly sisters. I mention it here because it is an example of how an old myth grows into contemporary relevance through the imagination of an individual expressing the unconscious need of his or her time.

However, the still more ancient myth of Demeter and Kore is a seedbed of feminine experience for women of all times and places, and I shall now try to explore some of its unchanging wisdom.

The story, taken from the Homeric Hymn to Demeter, is as follows.

Demeter's lovely daughter, Persephone (also called Kore) was playing with her companions in the meadows and, wandering off by herself, she saw a flower, a narcissus with one hundred blossoms, which Zeus himself with help of Gaia, goddess of Earth, had caused to grow as a snare for her. Fascinated by this flower, with its intoxicating scent, she reached to pick it. At that moment the earth opened, and the Lord of the Dead himself appeared from the depths with his immortal horses and, seizing her in spite of her

cries, carried her off to the underworld, unseen and un-
heard by any except the goddess Hecate who, as she was
thinking "delicate thoughts," heard the cry from her cave.
Otherwise only Helios the Sun himself witnessed the act.
Persephone cried out to Zeus to save her, but he took no
notice at all, for he himself had planned the whole thing.

The mountains and the depths of the sea, however, carried the sound of her voice, and "her lady mother heard
her." For nine days the sorrowing mother, the great goddess Demeter, wandered over the earth carrying burning
torches and stopping neither to eat nor to wash, but no one
anywhere could give her news of her lost daughter.

But on the tenth day came the goddess Hecate, bearing a
torch, and told the seeking mother that her daughter had
been ravished away, but that she had heard only and not
seen who the ravisher might be. Then together the two
goddesses went to Helios, the Sun, as he drove his chariot
across the heavens, and Demeter entreated him to tell her
what he had seen. He answered that Zeus himself had
given Kore to his brother Hades for his wife, and he urged
her to cease lamenting as this was a good marriage for her
daughter.

But her grief only increased the more and she wandered
unknown, and disfigured by sorrow, among the cities of
men, until she came one day to Eleusis and there she sat by
the wayside beside the Maiden's Well where the women
came to draw water. She bore the form of an old woman
past childbearing, and she sat in the shade of an olive tree.
Then came the four daughters of the King of Eleusis to
draw water, and when they saw her, they questioned her,
and she told them that she was far from her home in Crete
and sought for work—to nurse a child perhaps. Then the
princesses led her to their father and mother, for they
needed a nurse for a late-born son. With her dark robe and
her head veiled she came into the house of the king, and her
great height and the light which came from her struck awe
into them all. At first she sat sad and speechless, but the
ribald jokes of an old woman cheered her. When they of-

fered her wine, she refused it saying she was not permitted to drink it and asking for meal and water mixed. Then she took the child from his mother and held him "on her fragrant heart," and he grew daily stronger and more beautiful on food that was more than mortal. Each night she took the child and laid him in the fire like a brand while his parents slept. But one night the child's mother came in the night and saw what was being done to her child and cried out in terror and anger and snatched him from the goddess, thus depriving him of immortality. The goddess revealed her identity, upbraiding the mother for her "witlessness" in destroying the child's chance of immortality, and she ordered that a great temple be built for her there in Eleusis. When this was done she sat within the temple and mourned for her daughter.

Now she brought a terrible year on mankind, for she withheld growth from the earth, and no seed came up, and all the fruits of the earth were withering, so that mankind would surely have perished, and the gods would have been left without worshipers. So now Zeus in his heaven sent Iris to Demeter and begged and implored her to return among the gods and restore fertility to the earth, but she was deaf to all his pleading, even when each and all of the gods had come one by one to persuade her. And then at last Zeus sent Hermes to his brother Hades to tell him he must release Kore to her mother Demeter so that she might no longer withhold the seed from the earth.

Hades then turned to the still grieving Persephone and said that she might go, but offered her a pomegranate seed to eat as they parted. And she, though she had eaten nothing in the underworld, now, in her joy, took it and ate it, thus ensuring that she must return. Only if she had not eaten could she stay always with her mother. Henceforth she must return always to the underworld for one-third of the year. Then as they rejoiced in each other Hecate came again and kissed Kore many times and from that day was her "queenly comrade." And then Spring burst forth on the earth, but for one-third of each year the trees were bare and the land lay fallow. And as Demeter caused the grain to grow rich and fat again, she taught the meaning of it to all the rulers in Eleusis and gave instructions as to her rites, and the mysteries which should be celebrated there.

In his essay on the Kore [1] (the primordial maiden) Jung has said, "Demeter and Kore, mother and daughter, extend the feminine consciousness upwards and downwards—and widen out the narrowly conscious mind bound in space and time, giving it intimations of a greater and more comprehensive personality which has a share in the eternal course of things . . . It seems clear enough that the man's anima found projection in the Demeter cult . . . For a man, anima experiences are of immense and abiding significance. But the Demeter-Kore myth is far too feminine to have been merely the result of an anima projection . . . Demeter-Kore exists on the plane of mother-daughter experience which is alien to man and shuts him out."

There is an immense difference between the mother-son and the mother-daughter experience. On the archetypal level the son carries for the mother the image of her inner quest, but the daughter is the extension of her very self, carrying her back into the past and her own youth and forward to the promise of her own rebirth into a new personality, into the awareness of the Self. In the natural pattern of development the boy will feel his separateness from his mother by reason of his masculinity much sooner than the girl and will begin his striving for achievement. Everywhere, however, before the twentieth century, the growing girl remained at home contained in the orbit of her mother until the time came for her to become a mother herself and so reverse her role. Thus she would grow naturally from the passive state of being protected into the vital passivity of opening herself to receive the seed, the transition point being marked actually or symbolically by the violent breaking of her virginity.

Margaret Mead has written, "If women are to be restless and questing even in face of child-bearing they must be made so through education." For better, for worse, she has been made so. It can lead a woman either to disaster or to her great opportunity, and if she is to succeed in bridging the gap it is vital that, in one way or another, she pass through the Demeter-Kore experience in her inner life.

In ancient Greece the Eleusinian mysteries of Demeter bear witness to this overwhelming need of woman in her already growing separation from the natural pattern of the primitive feminine—the need for the Goddess to teach her the *meaning* of the deep transformation of her being from daughter to mother to daughter again. How much greater is that need today, when so often the woman lives almost like a man in the outer world and must find the whole meaning of her motherhood inwardly instead of physically, and when so many of those who do bear children are simply playing at "mothers and babies," never having allowed themselves to experience consciously the violent end of their daughter identification. There is strong evidence that the man initiated into the mysteries also "became" the *Goddess*, not the *God*. He too, in the flowering of Athenian civilization and the growing split between the conscious and unconscious, and between reason and the ancient goddesses of the earth and moon, must go through a profound anima experience and rediscover the meaning of the feminine within, must free his infantile anima from possession by the mother, and then find her again as mature and objective feeling, mother and maiden in one.

Persephone is playing with her companions in the eternal Spring, completely contained in her carefree belief that nothing can change this happy state of youth and beauty. Underneath, however, the urge to consciousness is stirring, and "the maiden not to be named," strays away from her fellows, and, intoxicated by the scent of a narcissus, she stoops to pick it and in so doing opens the door through which the Lord of the Underworld rushes up to seize her. We may notice here that Gaia, mother earth, is clearly distinguished from Demeter in this myth. She is Zeus's fellow conspirator as it were! Kerenyi says, "From the

Earth Mother's point of view, neither seduction nor death is the least bit tragic or even dramatic."

It is through the father that the daughter first becomes conscious of her self. When there is no adequate father-image in a girl's life, the identity of daughter and mother can assume a tremendous intensity, or else when the father-image is very negative and frightening, the daughter may unconsciously take on the mother's problem in a peculiarly deep way, sometimes carrying it all her life, long after the mother's death, and so remaining crippled in her effort to face her own fate in freedom. Normally the girl begins to detach from the mother, and to become conscious of her own potential motherhood through love of the father. Thus she is ready for the intoxicating moment of finding the narcissus—seeing *herself* as a person (as Narcissus saw his own face in the water), and the inevitable rape will follow. Dionysos was admiring himself in a mirror when he was set upon by the Titans and torn to pieces, the dismemberment which led to his rebirth. He is a male counterpart of Persephone.

The moment of breakthrough for a woman is always symbolically a rape—a necessity—something which takes hold with overmastering power and brooks no resistance. The arranged marriages of the primitive were often accompanied by a ritual stealing of the woman. The carrying of the woman over the threshold has survived through the centuries, becoming finally a joke, its connection with myth being lost. Any breakthrough of new consciousness, though it may have been maturing for months or years out of sight, comes through a building up of tension which reaches a breaking point. If the man or woman stands firm with courage, the breakdown becomes a breakthrough into a surge of new life. If he cannot stand it and settles for an evasion, then he will regress into neurosis.

The Lord of the Underworld is he who arises, bursts forth from the unconscious with all the tremendous power of instinct. He comes "with his immortal horses" and sweeps the maiden (the anima in a man) from the surface life of her childish paradise into the depths, into the kingdom of the dead—for a woman's total giving of her heart, of herself, in her experience of her instincts is a kind of death. This statement in no way equates this total giving with the outward experience of intercourse with a man. This is a normal part of it and by far the easiest way, but the instincts may be experienced to the full, sometimes perhaps even more profoundly, by a woman whose fate does not bring her the fruition of intercourse on the physical plane. An immature man may experience his instincts in a compartment, so to speak, without deep-seated damage—but not so a woman. If she does so she pays a very great price. It was not merely a man-made piece of injustice that condemned a woman's adultery as so much more shameful than a man's. The horrible cruelty of conventional prejudices should not blind us to the archetypal truths from which these distorted collective judgments spring. The woman who gives herself on the instinctual level without the love of her heart betrays the very essence of her being as woman. A prostitute, so called, whose warmth of *heart* flows out to the man in her every encounter is a far more moral person than the respectable wife who fulfills her "duty" with hidden hatred in her heart.

Persephone cries out in fear and protest as the cord of her tie to her mother, to her unconscious youthfulness, is violently cut, and nearby, Hecate, the goddess of the moon, hears her in her dark cave, though she does not see the abduction. There are three goddesses in the myth, Demeter, Persephone, and Hecate, and they are three aspects of woman. Hecate is the goddess of the dark moon, of the mediumistic intuition in woman of that which *hears* in the dark but does not see or understand. In this myth she appears as beneficent, linked positively to the others, but she has also of course her negative side. Disconnected from the other aspects of woman or from a man's undeveloped feeling she is the goddess of ghosts and witches and of the spells with which the unconscious binds us, or those near to us, from below. Mother earth and the sea, the mother of

all, also carry the sound of the daughter's voice, and Demeter, the mother, hears and knows that the daughter is lost
but not how. For nine days she wanders over the earth in
fear and sorrow, searching for her daughter but not *understanding*. She is wholly identified with her grief, swallowed
by it, even her body forgotten so that she does not eat or
wash. It is the beginning of the unspeakably painful struggle of a woman to separate from her possessive emotions,
the struggle which alone can give birth to love. As Demeter
sank into her grief, so every time we are shocked out of
some happy identification with another, which we have
fondly imagined to be an unbreakable state, we are beset
by the temptation to this surrender, to this despairing
search for that which has been lost, demanding that it be
restored to us exactly as it was, without any effort to discover the meaning of the experience. If we imagine we have
succeeded in restoring the status quo, then the whole story
will begin again and repeat itself endlessly and pointlessly
until we can follow the goddess to the next step—the dawning of her attempt to *understand*. This cut, this loss, must
be experienced by every woman both as daughter and as
mother or, especially in later years, as *both* at the same
time, for in every relationship between two women the
mother and the daughter archetypes are constellated; each
may mother the other, each may depend on the other and
ask to be mothered—the balance weighted now one way,
now the other.

At this point we will look at the specific experience of the
loss of the daughter in older women. It is the loss of the
young and carefree part of oneself, the opportunity for the
discoveries of meaning which are the task of the second
half of life: it is the change from the life of outer projection
to the detachment, the turning inward, which leads to the
"immediate experience of being outside time" in Jung's
words. In the language of this myth Death rises up and
takes away the woman's belief in everlasting spring. The
great majority of women today, having no contact at all
with the Demeter mystery, have extreme difficulty in giv-

ing up this unconscious clinging to youth, their partial identification with man's anima image, the unraped Persephone eternally picking flowers in blissful unconsciousness of the dark world below her. To such women the menopause brings long drawn-out disturbances of the body and the psyche as the conflict grows more acute and remains unresolved.

Kerenyi has written, "To enter into the figure of Demeter means to be pursued, to be robbed, to be raped" (as Persephone), "to rage and grieve, to fail to understand" (as Demeter), "and then to get everything back and be born again" (as Demeter and Persephone—the twofold single reality of Demeter-Kore). There can be no short cuts in this experience. All through her nine-day search (the symbolic nine of pregnancy) in her unconscious abandonment to grief the goddess had nevertheless carried burning torches in her hand, symbol perhaps of that small fire of attention which must be kept burning through the darkness of our journey when all meaning seems to have left us. On the tenth day Hecate, the hitherto dormant intuition came, also bearing a torch, and tells Demeter that her daughter had been ravished away, though she does not know who the ravisher may be. Demeter's moon nature brings the first rift in the isolation her absorbing personal grief has created. The stricken mother begins to intuit, to hear for the first time a voice which leads her to reflect upon that which has brought about her loss. She emerges enough from her self-concern to seek the aid of conscious reason. Together the two goddesses approach and question Helios, the sun, and he tells Demeter what has happened—that Zeus himself has arranged this marriage for her daughter and that this should be accepted as a good, a happy fate. But although her conscious mind has seen and understood, she cannot accept this reasonable answer. "She fails to understand" with her essential being and continues "to rage and to grieve."

Strangely enough, a woman is certainly right to reject this all-too-easy rational solution. "Let us be sensible," we say. "Our loss is good for us." Our grief was nothing but a childish reaction, and so on. Nevertheless the sun's calm reasoning has affected us. We must go on living. We must emerge from this totally self-centered, self-pitying, sorrow and be awake to other people. We must work, we must relate, but we must not deny our grief. And so Demeter comes to the well of the maidens at Eleusis—the place where the woman consciously draws the water up from the depths—and listens to the wisdom of the unconscious. There sitting under an olive tree she meets the king's daughters and offers to work as nurse to a child or at any menial task. No longer obsessed with *her* child, she can look again on the beautiful daughters of others and respond.

She goes to the palace. Arrived there she takes a lowly seat and her royal hosts offer her a cup of wine. But this she refuses and asks for a mixed drink of meal and water. It is not time yet for the wine of new life, the wine of full communion. We may remember here the words of Christ before his Passion. "I will not drink henceforth of the fruit of the vine until that day when I drink it new with you in my Father's Kingdom." There is a time when all seeking of release from tension must be refused, and the drink must be plain and tasteless.

The goddess remains deeply sad in her bearing and there follows the delightful image of the first smile appearing on her face as she listens to the crude jokes of Iamba, the serving woman. Her load is not lightened by some lofty thought, but by a most earthy kind of humor. The ancients were not cursed with the puritanical split between earth and the holy.

This then is the next step, after a loss, after any emotional blow, even after a seemingly trivial incident involving hurt feelings. We must return to the well of feminine wisdom. We can always work and we can always serve and we can recover our sense of humor, if we will descend far enough from our goddess-like superiority. Demeter here appears as a woman past child-bearing—she has lost her own child; she can never bear another in the flesh. Even the partial acceptance of this means that she can now give of her wisdom to the children of others. Demeter, being a goddess, has the power to bestow immortality, and she feeds the child of the King and Queen with inner wisdom, and at night she thrusts him like a brand into the fire which burns but does not consume.

What is the meaning of this incident for us? It can perhaps be seen from two opposite angles. The fear and the protest of the human mother is on the one hand a warning of how fatal to a child's inner life is the overprotective possessiveness of mother love which tries to prevent all suffering and danger from touching the beloved son. But from another angle, on another level, the human mother's instinct is surely right. This is a human baby and must grow up into a human being, subject to death. If he is to reach immortality, he must reach it on the hard road of human experience and the battle for consciousness—not be given immunity and deprived of the suffering and dignity of manhood by a goddess. She is right, as a mother's instinct so often is, even if for the wrong reasons. It may be noted that the goddess here descends to something like a temper tantrum, throwing the child heartlessly onto the floor and reviling the mother for her witlessness and for her lack of vision.

It could be that the goddess' behavior at this point gives us a glimpse into another danger of the way. After a violent awakening to loss, inner or outer, when already we have been greatly matured by this, and when we have, perhaps with great courage, decided to do our best to serve and to work, it is often a great temptation to seek assuagement for our anger and grief in the satisfaction of passing on to others who are still in a very unconscious state our hard-won wisdom, and then to get very angry when this priceless gift is refused.

In a woman, it would not be so much a matter of preaching ideas, but of being quite sure she can save someone else from having to go through the same agony. To feed the infant the food of divine wisdom is well, but to thrust him into the fire of premature transformation is to deprive him

of his choice as a human being. Many women do this
when they unconsciously lay on their sons the burden
of their own unlived inner quest, thrusting them inex-
orably into the priesthood or similar "spiritual" vocation at an early age. Of this particular child we are told
that all his life long the food of the goddess made him
wiser than other men, but thanks to his mother, he remained a man, retained his human fate and his human dignity.

As is the way with myth, this in no way invalidates the
other meaning—the danger of overprotection. There are
very few mothers who do not react as this one did when
they see the Great Mother, life itself, thrusting their
child—their outer or their inner child—into the fire. Only
when she herself will accept the Demeter experience is she
strong enough to consent to this. This is why the woman's
experience of the dark is so often expressed in myth by the
descent of the child, daughter or, more often, son, into hell.
It is a more terrible experience for the feminine psyche
than her own descent. The woman does not hang on the
cross. She stands at its foot and watches the torment of her
son. This is an image expressing the truth that immortality
can only be realized through the sacrifice of the most precious thing of all—and that for a woman is her child,
whether of the flesh or of the spirit. Christ was the Word
Incarnate and his life's work was mocked and spurned and
came to ignominious failure. Mary was the mother incarnate and her sacrifice was quite simply the complete acceptance of that which happened to her son, which meant
the death of every shred of possessiveness. Every archetypal story tells of course of the experience in its pure
form. It is the theme upon which the endless variations in
the individual psyche are built.

Demeter's effort to transmit immortality to the unconscious child may also be seen as an attempt at a short cut, if
we think of the child for a moment as her own new consciousness. After a partial awakening it is easy to imagine
that we have already arrived, or that the "baptism of fire"

can now take place immediately through some kind of miracle or through self-imposed, dramatic purging—that we won't need to suffer it through in actual experience over the years. Demeter has a long road to travel before she comes to the Holy Marriage of the mysteries and the birth of *the* divine child. Paradoxically it is the failure of this attempt to play the goddess and use her powers on the human child that recalls her to her true goddess nature. She remembers who she is, reveals herself, and immediately begins to prepare for the passing on of her vision, her essence, on an altogether different level—the symbolic level of the mysteries.

Demeter's center of gravity has changed, and she orders a temple to be built for her in Eleusis. It seems totally illogical that at *this* point she orders the temple to be built, for there is still a long road to be traveled before the opposites can be reconciled, before that which is to be worshiped and experienced at Eleusis is understood by Demeter herself. But myth, particularly feminine myth, is not logical. Its truth is of another order. Demeter has emerged from her wholly personal grief; she consciously knows that she is living a great mystery and that no matter how long her suffering may last, the end of it is certain. *The Heiros Gamos*, The Holy Marriage, which is the unity of all opposites, is an established possibility—she *remembers* her true nature. It is a moment of recognition, a kind of remembering of that which somewhere at bottom we have always known. The current problems are not solved, the conflicts remain, but such a person's suffering, as long as he or she does not evade it, will no longer lead to neurosis but to new life. The individual intuitively glimpses who he is.

So the goddess remembers herself and builds her temple, within which she now encloses herself, and in which she sits down again in a grief more terrible than before. It is not regression; it is her cave of introversion. Whereas at first she had simply surrendered to her sorrow, she now enters consciously into it. She is in a ritual, holy place, contained. She does not yet know the solution, but she herself must accept the dark, and inner death, if her daughter is ever to return to the light of day. And as the Goddess withdrew, so the earth dried up and withered, the sap of growth departed, and the land lay dying. The wasteland around the Fisher King in the Grail legend carries the same meaning—when it is time for a transformation of the whole personality, the birth of a totally new attitude, everything dries up inwardly and outwardly and life becomes more and more sterile until the *conscious* mind is forced to recognize the gravity of the situation, is compelled to accept the validity of the unconscious.

The gods now become frantic at what is happening on earth—pretty soon there will be no more men to worship the mighty gods of reason! As always happens, they get busy *bribing* Demeter to emerge from her temple and her sorrow—urging her to settle for a pleasant life of peace and honor on Olympus and to forget about her daughter down below, who can be left to keep the dark powers happy and prevent them from bothering the upper gods. So does reason and the fear of the dark speak to us. "Even if my greatest value does stay buried forever, it is foolish and arrogant of me to make so much fuss about it. I must conquer my misery, stop thinking about it, make the best of things as they are. Surely the great god Zeus must know best, and he is offering me ease and a position of great importance." But Demeter does not for a moment yield to good-sense arguments. There can be no half-way solution, no stopping at the state of separation of the opposites. She is deaf to all the entreaties and appeals of every god in turn. She uses the invincible weapon of the woman who, when something utterly irrational and against all conscious values rises up from the root of her being, simply sits still and refuses to budge. No man can resist this, but unfortunately we too often use this tool when we are moved not by a real intuition from our roots, but by our overpowering emotional possessiveness or an animus opinion.

The gods give in to Demeter, of course, and at last the conscious and the unconscious, the masculine and the feminine begin to pull together. It seems at first simply a capitulation of consciousness to the regressive longing of the mother. Zeus sends Hermes to tell Hades he must give Persephone back and restore the status quo, for Zeus himself cannot produce the solution which reconciles the opposites. Only when Hades the Lord of Death, Zeus's dark brother, will cooperate can the answer come. It is he who gives Persephone the seed of the pomegranate to eat—and she, who has hitherto rejected all food (refused to assimilate the experience), now in the moment when she is full of joy at the thought of not having to accept it, takes the pomegranate seed involuntarily, but voluntarily swallows it. In spite of her protests, she really has no intention of regressing to identification with her mother again. This is an image of how the saving thing can happen in the unconscious before the conscious mind can grasp at all what is going on. There are many dreams in which the dreamer tries to return to an old thing or situation but finds, for example, the doors barred or the telephone broken. The ego still yearns for the status quo, but further down the price has been paid, and we *can't* go back. Hence the great value of dreams in making us aware of these movements below. Even Demeter in her conscious planning, still half yearns for her daughter to return as before; but her questioning is quite perfunctory. As soon as she knows the seed has been eaten, there is no more said on the subject—all is joy. Persephone has eaten the food of Hades, has taken the seed of the dark into herself and can now give birth to her own new personality. So also can her mother. They have both passed through death to the renewal of a new spring—the inward renewal which age need never lose—and have accepted the equal necessity of winter and life in the darkness of the underworld.

The two become Demeter-Kore instead of Demeter and Kore. Now, to complete the unity, Hecate joins the others; she too is united to Persephone, becoming from that day her "queenly comrade," mother, maiden, and sibyl—the threefold nature of woman made whole. The images unite;

they no longer merge or fight or possess each other, and the woman who knows this experience becomes "one in herself."

The Mysteries

Demeter, united to her daughter, taught the rulers of Eleusis her rites and her mysteries, and these mysteries were for a thousand years a center of the inner religious life of antiquity. It is a measure of the power and depth of experience of the initiates that in all this time the secrets were never revealed by any one of the vast numbers involved. The merest hints leaked out, so that we can only know that certain symbols played a part, but very little about the rituals which led to the final revelation.

It is certain that the rites were not a mystery-drama, not an acting out of the story of the two goddesses, though each element of the myth was *symbolically* experienced. The initiates gathered in Athens on the first day—anyone could be a candidate if he spoke Greek and was not guilty of the shedding of blood—and went through a purification ritual of bathing in the sea. Probably they had already been through the lesser mysteries of Persephone at Agrai in which water and darkness played a major part, and the candidate experienced the passive suffering of the raped Persephone in the underworld through a conscious act of surrender. After the bathing there was a procession to Eleusis of the purified, bearing torches. Various symbolic actions were performed along the way, and on arrival outside Eleusis there was a time of fasting. The journey and the fasting were the symbols of Demeter's nine days of wandering and grief; Eleusis itself was the place of the *finding*.

It is probable that the rites proper began with a dance. Euripides wrote that on the night of the dance round the "fountain in the square of beautiful dances—the stormy heaven of Zeus begins to dance also, the moon and the fifty daughters of Nereus, the goddesses of the sea and the ever flowing rivers, all dance in honor of the golden-crowned maiden and her holy mother." Already the individual is lifted out of his small, rational, personal ego, and the whole universe is dancing with him.

There was also, it is thought, a communion drink—meal and water, probably, as drunk by Demeter in the king's hall, and the rites moved on through we know not what pattern to the climax of a ritual marriage by violence—not, as one might expect, that of Hades with Persephone, but the marriage of Demeter and Zeus. These are the mysteries of Demeter (not of Persephone, except insofar as she is an aspect of Demeter), of the Great Mother, whose experience of loss and finding led her to the *hieros gamos*, the union of the earth with the creator God, which means the birth of the divine child who is the "whole."

After the sacred marriage, a great light shone and the cry of the hierophant rang out "The great goddess has borne a sacred child—Brimo has borne Brimos." The goddess has acquired a new name which means "the strong one," "the power to arouse terror." Without terror, without experience of the terrible face of God, there can be no divine birth. It must be remembered that Persephone also, in her dark, negative aspect, is Medusa, the Gorgon's head, which she herself sends forth from the underworld—"a monstrosity," says Kerenyi, "the nocturnal aspect of what by day is the most desirable of all things." The birth of the child who bears the name, Brimo, alone can resolve the intolerable tension of these opposites, the child who is Demeter, Persephone, Hecate, Zeus, and Hades in one living image. The child is a boy, but also a girl, the androgynous fruit of the holy marriage. It is known that a single child initiate played a part in the mysteries, and that this could be either a boy or a girl, as the omens should decide.

The marriage and the birth, however, were not the final revelation. The most profound vision of all, the actual experience of immortality came in deep silence, when a mown ear of corn was held up and *seen* by the initiate. Nor can words ever accompany such an experience. The ancients said that at this point the idea of immortality "lost everything confusing and became a satisfying vision."

The mown ear of corn is a perfect symbol of immortality, of eternal rebirth. It is the fruit of life, the harvest, which feeds and nourishes, it is the seed which must sink into the earth and disappear in order to give birth again. It is mown down in the moment of its ripeness, as Persephone was mown down and torn from her mother, as every achievement in our lives outer or inner must be mown down in order to give birth to the new. It is the mother who nourishes, it is the seed of the father, and it is the child born of them both, in one image. The elevated Host in the Mass is the same symbol, the same silent epiphany, "showing forth" of immortality, with a tremendous added dimension. Bread is that which has been produced by man from the raw grain. *Consciousness* is added to the purely natural symbol, for Christ has consciously lived the myth. His initiates too must experience the mowing down, the burial and the rising again in a conscious realization of the Christ within. "Unless a corn of wheat fall into the ground and die, it remaineth alone, but if it die, it bringeth forth much fruit." That which must die is not the evil and the ugly but the thing of greatest beauty and meaning, the maiden of stainless innocence, so that we may finally know that over which death has no power.

There is evidence that the final act at Eleusis was the setting up of two vessels which were tipped over, so that the water flowed towards the east and the west, the directions of birth and death. Thus the ritual began and ended with water, symbol of the unconscious beginnings of all life and of the wise spirit of the conscious end—the living water "springing up into eternal life."

It should be stressed that the rites at Eleusis were neither an allegory nor a miracle but a mystery. An allegory exists in the realm of ordinary knowledge; it is a metaphor, a story, reflecting, for example, the cycle of the seasons or speaking of the living on of man in his descendants—facts which we all know of but which have for the most part, little power to affect or change our personalities. As

Kerenyi says, "There is a vast difference between knowing *of* something and knowing it and being it." Of the difference between miracle and mystery, he writes that a miracle causes people to talk endlessly about it, whereas the true mysteries are kept silent so that they may transform us from within through the symbols which in Jung's words "alone can reconcile the warring opposites, conveying to man in a single image, that which is thought *and* feeling and beyond them both."

The Homeric hymn ends with the words "awful mysteries which no one may in any way transgress or pry into or utter, for deep awe of the gods checks the voice. Happy is he among men upon earth who has seen these mysteries; but he who is uninitiated and who has no part in them never has lot of like good things once he is dead, down in the darkness and gloom." The ancient hymn thus asserts the three essentials of all the mystery rituals of all the religions. First, the rites must not be transgressed, altered in any way; second, they must be accepted without analysis and without question; third, they must not be spoken of, must be kept absolutely secret.

It is immediately obvious that modern man, even in the Roman Church which has been the guardian of the Christian mysteries for so long, is busy breaking all these essentials of a ritual mystery. We are changing it, we pry into everything, and we speak about it all incessantly. The element of awe is being deliberately banished. All this is not something which can or should be avoided. The growth of consciousness inevitably and rightly means that we pry into, we question everything with our hungry minds, and to try to stop this would be futile obscurantism. But it is equally futile and an arrogant folly to imagine that having banished the mystery from our outer cults, we can now dispense with it altogether. Then indeed, we shall end up in the "darkness and gloom" denying reality to the psyche itself and its truths. Without vision, without mystery, all of our fine intellectual understanding and its great values turn to dust.

The hymn refers to the fate of the initiate after death. In this context Kerenyi writes, "The 'eidola' in the realm of the dead . . . are the images with which the deceased individual, through his uniqueness, has enriched the world." Only to the extent that a man has lived his unique individual meaning does he attain to immortality. Persephone was called "the eternally unique" because she had united the two worlds, the dark and the light.

Surely the meaning of the dogma *extra ecclesiam nulla salus*, is that there is no salvation without experience of the mystery. It became a cruel and bigoted statement when it was interpreted in the literal outer sense (a kind of interpretation from which all the great dogmas of the Church have suffered immeasurably), and it gave sanction to such horrors as the Inquisition. The Ecumenical movement today is tackling this distortion on its own level with arguments of reason and good sense, but it misses the essential point, which is that man should recognize and experience the level of his being where this dogma is eternally and *individually* true. Outside the "Church," outside the mystery, there is no salvation.

When the outer cult loses its "mana" for a man, then the mystery falls into the unconscious and must there be rediscovered by the individual journeying alone in the dark places to the experience of the symbols within. When images of power and beauty rise up in dreams or fantasies, they make an immediate impact. We are in awe before them. Sometimes there comes a specific dream of initiation which may alter the whole course of a man's life. Such images are not something thought up or pried into, they cannot be altered, and instinctively we sense that they must not be spoken of except to another "initiate." When one does expose them wrongly, one can *feel* the power go out of them. Although their details are individual, unique, they link a man to the whole experience of mankind, and their impact can be immensely increased through a knowledge of the content and meaning of ancient myth, of the eternal themes which have embodied through the ages the truths of the human psyche. Our individual images may invoke perhaps, the dance of the primitive, or the flood or Demeter-Kore, Isis-Osiris, the Buddha's Flower sermon, the Zen Master's koan, and, for us in the West most powerfully of all, the birth and death of Christ, the bread and wine of the Mass. The analyzing mind which has destroyed mystery is thus linked again to the immediacy of the inner experience, and the redeeming symbol is reborn.

FIVE

Straw and Gold: Consciousness and the Mature Woman

Most people have heard of Rumpelstiltskin and have a vague idea that the story is concerned with the finding of a name, a theme so fascinating to humankind that it makes some impression even on the uninterested. There are many versions of the story but they differ only in details. It tells of a peasant girl whose father is continually boasting of her merits, even asserting that she has the power of spinning straw into gold. The King hears of this and sends his servants to fetch the girl, demanding that she spin some straw for him. When no gold appears, he shuts her up for a night, saying that, if the straw becomes gold by morning, he will make her Queen, but, if not, she will have her head cut off. She is in despair, her task being a human impossibility. Yet she is one of those who still know in their hearts that the impossible can happen, and so there appears a little man, who, when he hears her dilemma, rocks with merry laughter, since to him the job presents no problem at all. He will spin the straw into gold for her, but he exacts a price. When she becomes Queen, she must give him her first child. The girl accepts. She marries the King and has a child, and all is happiness until the little man comes to claim the child.

72

Then indeed she weeps and implores him for mercy, until finally he consents to let her off on one condition. She must find out what his name is. She guesses and guesses—every name she can think of or imagine. She sends servants far and wide to seek strange names, but all in vain. She is at the end of all hope when at the last moment a friend comes who has been walking in the forest and heard the little man singing to himself that his name is Rumpelstiltskin. So when he comes to the Queen for his final answer, she tells his name, and he is so furious that he grabs his foot and tears himself to pieces.

Fairy stories almost always have this character of "all or nothing"—reflecting a basic truth of the psyche. Tolerance is a major virtue, but like all virtues, it may be displaced from its proper level. It then turns into a soft, corrupting attitude blinding us to the basic "either-or" at the roots of life. In the imagery of the story, either we must turn the straw of our lives into gold, in which case we will marry the King, that is, find the royal creative meaning of our lives and bring forth our "child"; or, if we fail to do so, we will lose our heads, lose all possibility of coming to individual consciousness.

We should first think for a moment about the father's role in getting his daughter into this pickle. We are all very ready to go back and lay the blame for our troubles on our parents' blindness—and to recognize their mistakes is usually an essential step along the way. But, as we look deeper, we see that it is precisely to these mistakes that we owe the stimulus which forces us to seek the truth in our own way, if we will pay the price. The girl's father does a terrible thing to her because of his selfish pride. His guilt remains, but for her it is, we may imagine, the only thing which could have forced her to face the basic "either-or" and so launched her on her own unique and "royal" way.

How do we spin the straw of our lives into gold? Fundamentally it is a matter of a glimpse, a momentary, intuitive glimpse at this stage, of the ultimate truth beyond the opposites, that straw and gold are one thing. Who is the little man, coming from the unconscious where the opposites are one, without whom we cannot break through to this glimpse? For him the task is easy. He is a dwarf figure from under the earth, passionate and violent, wise and cunning, angry and merry, a creature of extremes, of childish affects, and to the young (or to the young part of us) he brings that breakthrough of passion, or romantic love, which turns the world to gold and makes the impossible possible. A boy or girl, if he or she is to plunge into life in any real way, *must* fall in love with someone or something. This does not refer of course to the easy, promiscuous, so-called "falling in love" which is mere appetite, but to the true romantic love, of which Charles Williams[1] has so beautifully written. This love is a glimpse of the ultimate glory, which cannot last in that form but is nonetheless valid and beautiful. "Unless devotion is given to the thing which must prove false in the end, the thing that is true in the end cannot enter." Devotion is the key word. The little man is that which releases in us a passionate devotion—to a person, to an idea, to an art—awakening in us that vivid perception of beauty in one thing which can transfigure the whole of our world to gold. Thus the little man brings that moment in a man or woman's life when he or she is committed without reservation to a love, a vision, a task, entering into life without thought of risk and accepting the basic "either-or." So one finds that the dirtiest bit of straw can turn to pure gold, and one is launched on the way that can lead over the years to maturity and the possibility of wholeness.

This little man, however, who comes to our help from the unconscious, is, as always with unconscious contents, an ambiguous figure. He is both friend and enemy, and, like Lucifer, he is both the bringer of light (*lucem ferre* means to carry light) and the threat of disaster. He brings to the girl the saving miracle, but he also exacts a price. The miracle will carry her to great happiness and success, but she must give up her child when he is born. So she makes a thoughtless promise, but it is also unconscious acceptance of future struggle. In accepting passion and the great release of energy it brings, we accept the resulting danger, and the price that is exacted is perhaps the one thing that prevents us from getting stuck in our infantile identification with our achievements. The romantic projection, so essential to youth, is extremely destructive in maturity, and so at the moment of the birth of the new, most precious value, comes the little man again, shaking us awake by threatening the child. "I saved you before; now give the child to me." This is most plainly seen outwardly in the contrast between the "romantic" possessive mother, emotionally identified with her child, and the creative mother, who nourishes her child and sets him free. The latter has found the little man's name.

We can watch this pattern not only in the span of a lifetime, but in the frequent ups and downs of the inner life. We experience a breakthrough of consciousness, the birth of a new potentiality demanding a new kind of commitment, and immediately we are tempted to romanticize this new vision, to possess and identify with it, which means that it will pass into the power of that ambiguous, emotionally unstable little man and sink again into the unconscious. Only on one condition can the child be saved, and paradoxically it is the threatener himself who offers the chance of salvation. We must consciously be able to *name* this elusive power within us.

There was once a British Broadcasting Company program called "Kafka, Rilke, and Rumpelstiltskin," in which Idris Parry defined Rumpelstiltskin in his unnamed state as "a confusion of boundless possibilities." Our way to maturity could be defined as a long and arduous effort to name these possibilities, to name our reactions and our complexes, so that instead of alternately being carried by them or drowned in them, we may find them a source of controlled strength. With the name there comes to us the power of detachment and of conscious choice.

The power of the *Name* is a great and holy theme in all religion and myth, in the whole history of consciousness. The name is the word, the symbol of that which separates

man from the beast, from unconscious nature, and with it
comes power. Adam named the beasts, and with the naming came his domination over them. Primitives are extremely careful about the speaking of names. If an enemy
knows a man's name, he automatically gains power over
him. Even today the signing of a man's name is an irrevoc-
able commitment, a handing over of power to someone
else.

In the Name of God resides his power. At baptism, which
is the ritual of entering into potential conscious union with
the Divine, a child is given his or her unique personal
name, "In the Name of the Father, the Son, and the Holy
Ghost." Man has through the ages believed that by speaking the name of God in purity of motive, we invoke the
light-giving power of the Spirit, and that in blaspheming
it, we set loose the destructive power of darkness. The fact
that these beliefs have lost their power in our culture in no
way lessens their deep meaning in the psyche.

There are "levels" of names. A person sometimes dreams
at a moment of great increase of consciousness that he has
been given a new name. T. S. Eliot has written, humor-
ously but nonetheless profoundly, of these "levels" in his
poem "The Naming of Cats." The cat must have an
everyday name in common use, a special name which is
hers alone, and finally a secret name.

These "levels" are just as applicable to man. We have our
family name, which any stranger uses; our unique, personal name only to be used by those close to us (one
symptom of the lack of respect for individuality in our society is the indiscriminate use of the personal name); and
finally that secret name which we seek consciously or unconsciously throughout our lives, the name which is
unique and yet one, we may believe, with The Name. "To
him that overcometh will I give to eat of the hidden manna,
and will give him a white stone and in the stone a new
name written which no man knoweth save he that re-
ceiveth it."

We know, then, that in approaching our own depths, we

are searching for the right names for the unseen forces within us. This is very far from arriving at a mere intellectual definition. It is the search for the true symbolic image in which we recognize the essence of the thing, a *word* in which the indefinable is expressed beyond intellectual categories. In the process of searching we bring to bear all the powers of intellect, imagination, feeling, and instinct, and then perhaps the name will become known to us as if by accident, arising spontaneously from the depths, bringing a new intuitive certainty, the word made flesh, the union of opposites.

So it was for the girl in the story. She searched and searched, tried every name her memory or imagination could conceive, sent her servants into far countries to seek for new possibilities. For us one powerful form of this seeking can be the use of active imagination. We can talk to the figures in our dreams, inviting them to reply to us, to reveal their characters and motives. It is not easy to do this, but the effort can be immensely rewarding, as it brings together the conscious and unconscious much more dynamically than mere conscious talk *about* a dream. However, at the last, the name will break through, usually at a moment when we feel that all our efforts have been in vain, and it seems to come by chance. Not so, of course.

Idris Parry's talk is largely concerned with the nature of so-called accidents. If the finding of Rumpelstiltskin's name is a mere accident, then, he says, "the whole thing is a swindle." But coincidence truly means "the falling together of events." He quotes Kafka: "Accident is the name one gives to the coincidence of events of which one does not know the causation."

This total relevance of everything that happens is what Jung calls *synchronicity*, what Charles Williams calls *co-inherence*, and what is truly meant by the *Will of God*.

Idris Parry asks what the girl had done to deserve her knowledge. The answer is "nothing." "It comes to her, she does not go to it, and she succeeds for that very reason," says Parry. Kafka says, "Stay at your table and listen.

Don't even listen, just wait, be completely quiet and alone. The world will offer itself to you to be unmasked." It is not, however, entirely true that she has done nothing. She has tried with all she has to find the answer, used all her faculties in a supreme effort, and so fulfilled the essential condition for being awake enough to hear the name when it is spoken. Through this effort alone can we come to the point at which we are *able* to be still and wait in the real sense. Kafka's words express great truth, but a very dangerous one if we interpret it on the wrong level. Sitting and waiting without having made every effort of which the conscious personality is capable would be merely a matter of sloth or evasion, suspiciously like waiting to be spoonfed. Always, however, we must remember that in the end the answer will be given, not earned. The real goal of all our efforts is to arrive at the capacity for this goal-less waiting. Then, indeed, the little man will sing his name, and the friend will "chance" to hear, and we shall break through to freedom and the "child" will be safe.

Why does the little man tear himself to pieces in the end? He is unbridled affect, convulsed with merry laughter, or screaming and dancing in rage. When he is named, these warring emotions in the Queen are resolved in the birth of true feeling, and they tear themselves to pieces harmlessly, as their energy passes into the new consciousness of the mature woman. It is a lesser fairy story image, perhaps, of the tearing to pieces of the god Dionysius, the dismemberment of the King in Alchemy, which is the prelude to rebirth. In the fairy story the self-destruction of Rumpelstiltskin means the safety of the "child," the new possibility of wholeness in the mother. In her new mature consciousness she no longer needs to spin straw into gold, for the passionate projection of images essential to youth has yielded to the objectivity of the free individual. Straw remains straw, gold remains gold; clear and distinct in their proper function, they no longer pass one into the other but unite in the infinite pattern of the whole. This is the final miracle.

SIX

Money and the Feminine Principle of Relatedness

The word *money* is derived from the Latin *moneta* meaning mint or money, and was originally the name of the goddess in whose temple in Rome money was coined. It is significant indeed that the goddess from whose temple, from whose womb, so to speak, sprang the coinage of our civilization has sunk into obscurity and is forgotten, while the money which was dedicated to her has acquired an ever-increasing autonomous power and is worshipped unashamedly as an end in itself.

It was certainly not by chance that the ancient Romans set their mint in the temple of a goddess and not of a god—for money is a symbolic means of exchange and therefore belongs to the feminine principle of relatedness. If, therefore, the "goddess" is missing, that third transpersonal factor which gives meaning to every exchange between human beings, whether physical, emotional, spiritual or financial, then we are in acute danger, for the thing or the experience has lost its connection with the symbol, the meaning sinks into the unconscious, and we are inevitably possessed by some kind of autonomous, power-filled complex. Thus the love of the divinity at the heart of exchange turns into the love of money itself which, in the words of Timothy in one of his epistles, is "the root of all evil."

79

Money itself is not, of course, evil. It is an essential for any kind of civilized society; but the minute our attitude to money is divorced from its meaning as an exchange between people involving *feeling* values, then we begin to love money for its own sake or for the sake of that which we can gain from it, either possessions or security or, worst of all, power. It hardly needs to be added that to maintain our sense of the symbol in our money dealing requires of us a very high degree of consciousness indeed.

Charles Williams, in one of the poems in his Arthurian cycle, wrote of the beauty inherent in the simple exchange of goods and services and described the coming of the coins which were to symbolize it. The poem is called "Bors to Elayne: The King's Coins." [1] Sir Bors is married to Elayne in this poem, and he sings of the beauty of her hands as she bakes bread to feed the men who have been working in the fields. He particularly stresses the thumbs, the unique feature of the human hand ("the thumbs are muscled with the power of good will"), and we feel them as the symbol of that conscious exchange by which human beings truly live. In this exchange, Bors says, *"none only earn and none only pay."* Elayne, the lady, kneads bread with her thumbs. The beautiful meaning of the word *lady* is, in fact, "kneader of bread." The men sow and harvest the wheat; thus they both earn and pay for the bread by their labors, as Elayne and her women, by their work of baking and distributing the bread, both earn and pay for the wheat and the labor of the men. It is, as C. S. Lewis says, "the honourable and blessed" exchange of one kind of service, one kind of work, for another.

Bors, however, has come from London where, with the growth of civilization, a new means of exchange has come into being. "The king has set up his mint by Thames. He has struck coins." Bors knows that this is a necessary thing, but he has been having bad dreams. The coins have the King's head on one side and a dragon on the other. It is as though already they have acquired a life of their own, these little dragons, and the king's head (the royal consciousness

of the Self, in symbolic language) is dead. The "dragonlets
. . . scuttle and scurry between towns and towns," / their
eyes "leer and peer, and the house roofs under their weight
/ creak and break"[2] in Bors' dream. Kay, the king's stew-
ard, the businessman of Arthur's court, says, "Streams
are bridged and mountains of ridged space / tunnelled;
gold dances deftly across frontiers. / The poor have choice
of purchase, the rich of rents . . . Money is the medium of
exchange."[3] Taliessin, the king's poet, however, is afraid.
His hand shakes when he touches the dragons. "I am afraid
of the little loosed dragons. / When the means are autonomous, they are deadly; when words / escape from verse
they hurry to rape souls; when sensation slips from intellect, expect the tyrant."[4]

The Archbishop in the poem replies that even when God
is hidden, the truth of exchange remains. I take him to
mean that an individual may still hold to the symbol no
matter what collective values prevail. He goes on, "We
must lose our own ends . . . my friend's shelter for me, mine
for him . . . the wealth of the self is the health of the self
exchanged . . . Money is a medium of exchange."[5] The difference between the Archbishop's statement and Kay's is
profound. "Money," says the Archbishop, "is *a* means of
exchange" (for each person)—not "the medium of exchange."

Bors ends with a question to his lady and a prayer. Compact, he says, is becoming contract; and he adds that man
now *only* earns or *only* pays. Then he asks, "What without
coinage or with coinage can be saved?" He ends, "Pray,
mother of children, pray for the coins."[6] It is not the coinage itself which is the issue; the evil is the loss in man of the
link to the feeling values of exchange. Therefore it is the
"mother" who must pray—the woman whose very being
depends on relatedness.

A compact is, literally, an agreement based on feeling
values; it means a coming together in peace, *cum pace*. A
contract is a legal or financial agreement which binds outwardly, regardless of the human feelings involved. So

when compact becomes contract within us, men begin to earn without paying or pay without earning, and money is divorced from the meaning of exchange.

If we hold one gold or silver coin in our hands and really see it, what a beautiful thing it is. If we still used gold coins stamped with the king's head on one side and the dragon on the other, it would surely be easier to feel with joy the symbolism of the Self in every earning and every paying. (I have one gold coin still—a 1910 half sovereign with the king's head and St. George with the Dragon.) Even our debased coinage retains vestiges of the importance of the symbols, reduced to mere signs though they may be—the great man's head and the eagle of the 25¢ piece, for instance—and all coins have the roundness of the whole. Our paper money is a mere convenient token of true money; it still has the head, but the pictures of public buildings which replace the old animal symbols betray the poverty of our attitudes. The dragons have indeed escaped, and in the unconscious they make an unholy alliance with the sterile severed head; thus men watch helplessly the "leering and peering" of the loosed power. "When the means are autonomous they are deadly." When words escape from poetry, when the mint emerges from the Temple, then souls are raped; speech becomes jargon, paying becomes bribing, earning becomes joyless necessity, and the acts of exchange which are the glory of humanity become mere bargains. (*It would be hard to say whether words or coins are ahead nowadays in the race to destroy souls.*)

That good old English word *stock* has many beautiful meanings, all derived from the original one of the main trunk of a tree or plant onto which grafts are made. It means too the store of raw material, of goods which are the basis of new development. "He comes of good stock" we say, speaking of a man's roots—of the raw material of his inherited personality. When autonomous money becomes the stock upon which the life of a man or a society is grafted, the rot begins. We forget the ancient and beautiful image of the market place, where fruits of the earth and products of the human hand were exchanged, when we talk of the money markets and stock exchanges of the world. In these money is made to breed and breed only itself. People buy and sell rye or wheat, for instance, without the remotest connection with the crops growing in the fields, even in thought. Something is to be had for nothing by the clever playing of the markets, and this is the absolute negation of exchange. The Usurers in Dante's Inferno were deep in Nether Hell on the sterile burning sand. One commentator has written that they were there because they made money breed—money, which is in itself sterile.

Under this weight of paper and the inflation it brings, our rooftops are indeed creaking and breaking. This "brood of carriers," as Taliessin calls the little loosed dragons, bring power to their owners, power and more power, until the good stock from which they sprang is wholly forgotten and people would think us crazy if we reminded them in this context that the word *share* had a blessed human meaning.

Money was a most wonderful invention of the human mind. It brought to man an enormous extension of freedom from the immediate necessities of mere existence. "The poor have choice of purchase, the rich of rents." At every step along the way of civilization energy was set free by money, and people could choose how they would spend this energy. They could and did choose creation, discovery and growth of all kinds. But in more and more people, the desire to possess the gold lured that energy to itself and the severed head, and the greed of the dragon overran the values of the heart and spirit.

Modern humankind is increasingly aware of this terrible predicament. There have been countless genuine and courageous efforts to counteract this autonomous breeding. The revolutionaries have attempted to solve the problem by a complete overthrow of personal ownership—only to create the worse horror of the manipulation of the money forces by a heartless all-powerful state for the so-called good of the many, and the concentration of this tremendous power in the hands of a very few.

Democracies, with varying success, and in spite of their muddles and corruptions, have tried to find a means of controlling the greed of the few, caring for the old and sick and unfortunate, searching, at least, for a social equity which will not destroy individual freedom of exchange. But they have proved powerless to stop the breeding, the inflations and depressions.

Groups of individuals have sought to free themselves by pooling all their money and living in communities. But most of the members are not inwardly free from the greed which they seek to combat and are not yet capable of free exchange, so their well-meant efforts are an escape, not an affirmation. One cannot go back to the simple life until one has taken up the responsibility for money and learned the nature of exchange through both earning and paying. I do not believe that any commune can survive for long in our times when money is pooled. Religious communities through the centuries thrived because of the dedication which meant an inward earning and paying through an intense devotion to the symbolic life, but in our day individuals must increasingly take up their lonely responsibilities, and the temptation to escape from these through so-called community is very strong.

The lonely hermits were forerunners in the desert of what eventually a conscious person had to achieve *inwardly*. But no person today may legitimately renounce money outwardly until he or she has a true understanding of what inner poverty is. If money is *taken* from someone, then he is tested indeed; for the very poor it is as difficult as for the very rich to hold to the values of true exchange.

It is a very great thing that so many young people today are seeing clearly the horrible evils of a money-dominated society. Their danger is that, in so rightly rejecting its values, they may also reject the responsibility for that which money symbolizes—the earning and paying for which it stands. They speak of and indeed show love and concern for each other, but too often the "love" is confined to those of like mind and like age—and is therefore merely an extended self-concern. Exchange is never exclusive. Moreover, the insidious belief may creep in that "society" owes them a living—that money *itself* is evil. Therefore, they feel anything can be demanded or even stolen from others, especially from impersonal organizations, without obligation either to earn or to pay. This, of course, is as complete a denial of human exchange as any of the financiers are guilty of.

What, then, is the answer for the ordinary citizen, aware of the evils, but seemingly powerless to alter anything? As with every other collective problem, there can be no outer solution without the transformation of individuals. There is, therefore, the imperative need for each person to enter upon the hard way of scrutinizing with ever-increasing consciousness his or her own personal attitudes to money.

So let us look closely at some of the signs whereby we may recognize in our ordinary transactions either the symbol at work or the insidious power, greed or fear born of the autonomy of money within us.

We may begin by considering the very common pitfalls into which married couples fall, not because married people are any more unconscious than anyone else, but simply because marriage between a man and a woman is the greatest of all human symbols of exchange between the two basic forces of the universe—the creative and the receptive, the male and the female, the head and the dragon. Therefore the money dealings between the partners in a marriage are apt to show up very clearly their conscious and unconscious attitudes towards the meaning of exchange. I am inclined to say that married people who are seeking consciousness are extremely lucky in having this clearly defined problem to work on! Of course people living alone have exactly the same attitudes to contend with, but it is very much easier for them to bury the whole thing and imagine that they are not at all unconscious about money

matters. Even friends living together and sharing expenses
are not forced to confront at every turn the age-old assumptions in the unconscious about husbands' "rights," or
the modern emergence of women's "rights." A single person usually has his or her own money and responsibilities,
but it would be good for every unmarried person to think
deeply about how he or she would feel about money in the
event of marriage. It is not by chance that Williams' poem
begins with that beautiful imagery of the essence of exchange between Bors and his wife Elayne—between his
men and her women—the collective exchange, be it noted,
springing from the individual one.

There are several symptoms of the betrayal of exchange
in marriage. First there is the old and still very powerful
male assumption, in spite of all protestations to the contrary, that he, being the chief money provider, owns all the
money and will give to his wife sufficient for her needs.
Usually he will say or imply, "I can't understand what she
is fussing about. She can have anything she wants within
my means. She knows that." He does not see the power
motive at the back of this. He will be the bountiful giver.
He is most willing to pay for his wife's pleasure, but he
does not really admit that she earns and pays by her work
and her childbearing and her love and that she needs to feel
that she has money which is *wholly* her own, so that she
may choose her ways of spending without reference to him
should she so wish. Let it be added that often the woman's
unconscious is equally to blame with its tendency to welcome absorption into another's life. A woman so often
takes the easy way of complaining instead of standing up
for her values (not rights), so deep is the inherited sense of
inferiority with its temptation to avoid all responsibility.
Quite often, too, the opposite may happen. The man refuses
all responsibility and hands over the management of their
joint money to the woman. She doles it out to him. The
animus may be delighted, but woe to the chances of exchange in that marriage.

More common in our time, and particularly in the first

warm and genuine sharing of a new marriage, is the decla-
ration by both man and woman, "We shall pool all we have
in a joint account and have no disagreements about how it
shall be spent." It may well be so, but these people with all
their manifest good will reckon without the immensely
powerful symbolic meaning of money itself. It means
exchange—it does not mean mixing. If the two people concerned have really arrived at a very high degree of the
inner separation which is individuation, all well and good;
but I need hardly say that such a situation is extremely
rare. For almost all there is a hidden danger which over the
years can undermine a potentially fine and growing
partnership. One question usually opens a person's eyes.
Have you thought that in making this arrangement you
effectually destroy any possibility of every truly giving
your wife or husband a present? The question may sound
superficial—in fact it lays bare the whole deadly business
of how we are misled by so many seemingly generous im-
pulses to the evasion of the responsibilities of individual
exchange. Sooner or later it is a hundred to one that the
partners will begin to feel, unconsciously if not consciously, either a resentment because he wants something
and is not free to buy it, or a guilt that she has spent money
which was not wholly hers.

A joint account for joint expenses which can be budgeted
is obviously excellent; for the rest, unless each partner has
complete individual control of his or her share, without
obligation even to tell the partner what he or she does with
it, the dignity of exchange is easily lost.

When the woman has or earns money of her own and
retains control of it, things are easier, given the essential
good will. But if one or the other partner has much more
money than is needed for a moderate standard of living,
then other dangers arise. A woman's animus, operating out
of seemingly clear-cut principles, as he is apt to do, and
unconscious of his power drives, may insist on 50/50 pro-
ceedings when it is quite unsuitable. A man's anima may
fog everything up and obscure his power motives so that all

the true issues are lost. Each person in this challenging quest for the true nature of exchange must take into account the state of consciousness of the other and discover where to stand up and where to let go. There are no rules; the only vital thing is the fundamental honesty of the will to exchange, to earn and to pay—the refusal to dominate, to depend or to mix. If we do not do this in money matters, we most surely don't do it elsewhere.

In the area of wages and salaries, the issue is clear. When there is true exchange between employer and employed it is a beautiful thing—the master respecting the skills and service of the man, the man respecting the master's knowledge and willingness to take responsibility and risk. It can still today be a relationship full of that dignity and true equality so easily lost the minute everyone starts fighting for their "rights" instead of *for the fairness of exchange.* As soon as earning and paying become bargaining, the issues turn ugly; the love of money in both employers and employees takes over as an end in itself. Thus the meaningless spiral of inflation continues. The word *inflation* in this context means the blowing up of the artificial value of money disconnected from the goods it represents. The financiers see this entirely in an outer sense; it is in fact a symptom of the ever-increasing gap between money and its root in the ground of human relatedness.

The only thing we can certainly do about it is to give a great deal of attention to our individual attitudes when we employ anybody (even if it be a single cleaning woman), and when we are employed. Is our payment to an employee also an earning of his service on the feeling level? When we accept our earnings, have we really paid in full for them, and do we recognize the work of our employers which has earned the payment he makes to us? It grows more and more difficult, of course, to hold to these things in proportion to the size of the business or the institution, when employers are entirely unknown as people and have no notion of who their employees are. Nevertheless, what an enormous difference the attitude of the man at the top has on even a big organization. It creates an atmosphere by which even the most obscure employee will be influenced. One can usually tell by the atmosphere of a store whether the owner cares for the values of exchange in his money dealing or whether he cares only for money itself.

Of course, no matter what the general state of affairs is, one may come across individuals anywhere in whom this beauty shines. I suppose every woman among us can remember instances on her shopping trips when she has been served by a saleswoman who is truly concerned, not just to sell her any old thing, but to find the coat, or the dress that is exactly right, and this is accomplished for obviously personal as well as business reasons. We come away not only delighted with our acquisition but with a feeling of real exchange between people, and the money which passes is for the moment truly connected to that for which it stands. *In our hearts Elayne has baked bread for the reapers of the grain.*

The enormous size, however, of so many corporations and institutions is as nothing to the size of the State, that abstract entity to which we pay our taxes and on which we for the most part can safely vent the resentments and guilts born of our own unfaced shadow qualities—our own evasions of the responsibilities of true exchange. People who would cry out in horror when a man cheats his neighbor or refuses to pay his debts may grin when telling you how they have just hatched up a new plot to evade taxation. I am not, of course, talking about the many entirely legitimate ways of reducing one's tax load. That would be foolish sentimentality and scrupulosity. There is a thin line between that and dishonesty, but for anyone who thinks of money as a symbol of exchange, it can be a very clear one. If we really think deeply, taxation emerges as one of the greatest ideas that humankind has ever conceived. It is the means whereby people live in community with each other while still retaining freedom of choice in most of their spending and earning. Without taxation there must be dictatorship or anarchy. As on all levels of exchange, the sacrifice of a degree of freedom ensures the essential freedom.

The tax evaders, who often produce lofty motives for their actions, reply that since they disapprove so strongly of the ways in which the government spends public money, they will evade as much as they can. Could any reasoning be more specious? Do we refuse to pay a debt because we disapprove of the way our creditor spends his money? Our taxes are the debt which every man who lives in a civilized society owes to every one of the millions of his fellow citizens. It may be replied that we do not incur this debt willingly. Most surely we do, whenever we post a letter, use a road, accept a penny of welfare or unemployment money, or call the fire department or the police.

As to the often unjust, mistaken and corrupt ways in which tax money is spent, it is we, each one of us, who carry the final responsibility for the government in power, whichever way we have voted; for it has been truly said that a country has the government it deserves; that is, the government is a reflection of the dominant attitudes in the lives of its individual citizens. Whoever we vote for, if in our personal lives we do not adhere to the honesty and feeling values of true exchange in all our earning and paying, including our tax paying, then we are contributing most effectively to the greed and hatred and power-seeking which produce such things as militarism and the corruption of "lobbies." It is futile to fight such things if one is all the time practicing them under cover of righteous indignation, and the very last way to stop them is to withhold that which is a great affirmation of every human being's responsibility for all his fellows.

If a person believes that the government has betrayed the trust of the people he has, in a democracy, many means of fighting. If he or she is convinced that only rebellion will serve, then let him or her refuse all money payments and go to prison or leave the country.

Our dealings with impersonal entities such as the State, corporations, institutions and businesses can provide us with a searchlight into many of the unnoticed shadows within us—think, for instance, of the insidious temptations of the expense account, a most safe and easy way to defraud—safer even than semi-conscious money exchanges with one's parents or wife or husband or children. The State and the corporation are not pure abstractions; behind them all are individual people, no matter how hard it may be to imagine this. If we lose track of the clear beauty of exchange in our attitudes to these collectivities, we may be very sure there is something wrong in all our relationships—in all the closest and most valued exchanges of our lives.

Perhaps the most universal fear in us all is *the fear of the loss of security*. The smallest knowledge of the psyche awakens us to the fact that only by facing this fear and by giving *a fundamental consent to insecurity*, in any context, can we hope to know real freedom from anxiety. This is as true in relationships to money as it is to everything else. Anxiety about money is in no way dependent on the amount of money a person possesses. It is often much stronger in those who have plenty of money than in those who have little. It is in truth especially hard for the rich (and not only the rich in money) to enter the peace of the "Kingdom of Heaven," whose very definition is "exchange" on earth, because to do so we must accept, embrace even, insecurity on every other level of being, a thing which the rich (even the rich in spirit) often fear more than anything.

"The wealth of the self is the health of the self exchanged," says the Archbishop in Williams' poem. The word *health* is derived from the same root as wholeness. Only awareness of this can save us from the pursuit of security, possessions, and, finally, power through money as an end in itself. "When the means are autonomous they are deadly."

When we dream about money, it is often clearly a symbol of psychic energy. We may learn a lot from our dreams of money as to how we are spending our inner energy—whether we hoard it, make bargains with it, steal energy from others, or earn and pay in the freedom of exchange.

Finally we may think about the free giving and free taking of money. To give it or take it without any unconscious strings attached is no easy thing, and on one level it appears that we have to free ourselves absolutely from any thought of earning or of paying when we make a gift or receive one. The giver must have no ulterior earning motive; the gift must not buy goodwill; the recipient must never feel it is payment for value personally given.

There is, however, another level upon which any free giver or taker is most precisely and accurately earning and paying. It is the level from which Christ spoke when he said, "Owe no man anything but to love one another." In all our money dealing we symbolically incur and pay this universal debt if only we will dare to be aware of it. When we are thus aware, we shall give instinctively neither too little nor too much. Indeed, perhaps we could sum up this whole matter by saying that when in every money exchange we *both* earn and pay, pay and earn, then our earning and paying become the free giving and free taking whereby money enters the "Temple" once more, and the dragons are at peace with the head of the King in the pure gold of the human heart.

SEVEN

The Revenge of the Repressed Feminine

We look back from our peak of civilization on the blood feuds of the primitive as at something long outgrown. The impersonal retribution of the law has taken the place of private vengeance, but the instinctive demand for a death to pay for a death remains as alive as ever in the psyche, however sincerely we may consciously accept the obligation to forgive.

Before considering further the working of the revenge instinct in our own lives, we shall look at one of the great dramas of antiquity, and the three plays, called the *Oresteia*, by Aeschylus, which not only show the tragedy of human beings caught in this passion, but point forward to the possiblity of its ultimate redemption. The trilogy was written in the 5th century B.C. at the zenith of Athenian culture and is a drama of the Greek heroic age at the end of the Trojan wars. The first two plays are concerned with the endless chain of blood for blood, but at the end of the second play, *The Libation Bearers*, the action shifts from the outer world to the inner, with the appearance of the Furies, the Eumenides. In the third play, Aeschylus imagines the beginnings of human impersonal justice, which will replace the blood feud, and then goes beyond this to another dimension and the recognition that impartial justice and reason can never be enough to end the rule of "an eye for an eye." There must also be a reconciliation of the opposites in the realm of the gods—that is, for us, in the realm of the unconscious.

The story begins long before the opening of the first play, *Agamemnon*, with the seduction of the wife of Atreus, King of Argos, by Thyestes, the king's brother. Atreus took revenge on Thyestes by inviting him to a banquet in pretended forgiveness, and then, having killed Thyestes' children, he served them up to him to eat. Only one child escaped, Aegisthus, who returned to the court of King Agamemnon (Atreus' son), nursing thoughts of revenge. Ten years before the play opens, the abduction of Helen, wife of Menelaus, Agamemnon's brother, had led to the Trojan war of revenge against Paris, Prince of Troy, a war which decimated Greece and ended with the total destruction of Troy and its population. The third cause of the tragedy in *Agamemnon* was the sacrificial killing by the king of his own daughter, Iphigenia, at the time when the Greek army was held back from sailing to Troy by unfavorable winds and the gods demanded a human sacrifice. This act had turned Clytemnestra's great love for her husband, Agamemnon, to bitter resentment and hatred. To the mother, no religious reason could redeem the horror of that killing.

Agamemnon begins in the city of Argos, where all wait for news from Troy. Clytemnestra, the queen, has governed the city for ten years, with the strength and wisdom of a man, but Aegisthus has come home from exile and has become her lover, thus feeding her already passionate resentment against her absent husband with an added motive for his destruction. Aegisthus is an effeminate creature, and though he joins in the plot against Agamemnon, he keeps well out of the way when it comes to action. News comes of the fall of Troy, and the king returns in triumph, but it is an empty one in spite of big words. The flower of Greek manhood is dead, there are very few survivors, and we feel the full horror of the enormous price in human life and misery which has been paid for the paltry end of re-

venging one man for the loss of his wife. Agamemnon
brings with him Cassandra, the captive Trojan princess,
who is his mistress (allowed to Greek warriors in war).
Here is yet more fuel for the fire of Clytemnestra's resentment, and she is bitterly jealous. For she both loves and
hates Agamemnon and will kill the thing she loves. He has
betrayed her as mother; now he betrays her as wife. She
meets Agamemnon with simulated joy and flattery. He asserts his freedom from undue pride but really swallows her
flattery, and the symbol of this is his walking on the robe
she has spread on the ground for him, and with which she
is about to trap him. He enters the house, and while he is in
the bath, she entangles him in the robe and stabs him to
death.

The audience waits outside with the chorus. Clytemnestra emerges. She dominates the play, and one is some-
how compelled to respect her as she takes full responsibility for her deed. Like all avengers, she claims to have
carried out a *cleansing*. "Now all is paid and men may live
in peace," is their cry. Orestes is to make the same claim in
the next play. But the bloodshed in revenge begets another
revenge and so on without end.

In *The Libation Bearers*, the second play, Orestes, son of
Agamemnon and Clytemnestra, who had been sent away
from home as a child, before his father's return, has grown
up and returns to avenge his father. He meets Electra, his
sister, at Agamemnon's tomb, to which she has brought
libations. Together they plot to kill Aegisthus and Clytemnestra, their mother. They have to whip up their courage
for this worst of all crimes, telling themselves it is a cleansing of evil, casting themselves into a fury of self-pity and
finally putting the blame on the gods; for the Delphic oracle of Apollo has ordered Orestes to kill his mother. Face to
face with her, however, he still hesitates. The love between
them almost defeats the mutual hatred and fear. For we
know that she would have killed him out of fear and in
spite of love, just as he will kill her out of hatred. The
memory of the oracle tips the scale and he stabs her.

"Now," he cries, "I will take my rightful kingdom and rule in peace; all is cleansed." The triumph is shortlived. Remorse invades him and immediately the Furies appear, the avenging spirits of the Mother, and he runs from his kingdom to wander, homeless and terrified. Revenge has passed from the outer to the inner world.

In *The Eumenides*, the third play, the issue is first between man and the gods and finally between Apollo, the god of reason, and the dark instincts of the unconscious. Orestes' personal murder of his mother may be seen as a symbol of the murder by man's growing consciousness of his primitive identity with the unconscious world of the instincts. The Furies were not activated by any of the other murders—by the husband murder, the horrors of the war, not even by the horrible killing of the children. Matricide is in another category, the unforgivable crime in the eyes of nature.

The Furies were those terrible goddesses whose hair was writhing snakes, but most strangely their name, the *Eumenides*, actually means the Kindly Ones. It is one of the great paradoxes. Revenge is the chief characteristic of the witch, the rejected and repressed side of the feminine image, and we may notice that *every one of the crimes in this story is set in motion by a betrayal of woman, of the true feeling values.* The seduction of Atreus' wife and of Helen, Agamemnon's unnatural sacrifice, Clytemnestra's infidelity, all culminate in *the murder of the mother, the symbol of the rejection of great Mother Nature herself.*

Athens in Aeschylus' day was in fact moving into a dangerous split from the feminine values of nature, a split which in our day has reached terrifying proportions, and the wisdom of Aeschylus is more than ever valid for us. In *The Eumenides* he is little concerned with Orestes' personal story and sees the issue in depth as a problem of all mankind. The gods are the protagonists—there is no hope at all for a solution unless a mediator can be found; Apollo and the Furies, reason and instinct, would forever remain implacable enemies. In the play this mediating function is personified in Pallas Athene, who was for the ancient Greeks the symbol of masculine courage and understanding united to feminine feeling and instinctive wisdom.

Orestes, seeking sanctuary at Delphi with Apollo (who can at least send the Furies to sleep when he is around but can never drive them away), is sent by him to Athens to appeal to Athene. Reason in the Greeks was still in touch with the unconscious (Apollo spoke through the Sybil at Delphi) and therefore knew the need for a mediator, whereas nowadays reason all too often becomes rationality, which simply dismisses feminine values as nonsense. The Furies follow Orestes, breathing threats, and Athene's first response to her supplicant is to call a jury of citizens to try Orestes. Law is to be substituted for blood feud. Orestes admits his crime and pleads justification by his mother's wickedness and Apollo's explicit order. The Furies say that nothing whatever can excuse matricide. The jury is equally divided, and Athene gives her casting vote for Orestes. Civilized objective thinking can stop the chain of revenge on the outer level, but Athene very well knows that this can also result in driving the conflict underground where it will do far greater damage. Therefore, while her masculine judgment speaks for Orestes, she knows in her feminine wisdom that the Furies are also right and must be accepted. Apollo had rejected them utterly, identifying them with evil and everything regressive, emotional, uncivilized. It is as though Athene penetrates to the inner meaning of the Delphic oracle. It is true that man must free himself from the devouring mother who murders the values of consciousness, but not by means of another murder. Real freedom can only come through accepting inwardly the furies of instinct without loss of conscious values, thus redeeming them.

The Furies now utter horrible threats. They will poison the crops of the Athenians, bring disease and misery on all. Athene speaks to them gently, with persuasion, with respect. She knows that, if civilized justice and reason become identified with the Apollonian values as the only good, the destructiveness of the ancient mother goddesses will erupt in untold evil for mankind. The "murder" of the instinctive and the irrational by civilized consciousness will result in the final poisoning of everything, in outbursts of fury and killing on a collective scale infinitely worse than the personal blood feud, as we, today, so very well know. Athene, therefore, on behalf of her citizens, offers the raging goddesses acceptance and love. Aeschylus calls them "the ancient children," for they have the ruthlessness but also the spontaneous vitality of the child, and this a man rejects to his own undoing. If they in turn will accept this offer, absorb their anger in the nourishing aspect of their nature, then men will worship them in love instead of fear. They will preside over fertility in all its forms, the true function of the mother image. Instead of wandering in the dark, outcast, preying on the unconscious of man, they will have a place in every home, bringing richness to the crops, happiness in marriage, good fortune in childbirth— nourishment, in fact, to all the life-giving forces of nature. At first they will not believe Athene, but finally they are won over, as they always are when a man will face their terrifying power with the respect and acceptance of Athene. They exchange their snake headgear for green olive branches and the citizens lead them to their new home with a beautiful song, which ends the play.

So far does Aeschylus take us. He shows what must happen if civilization is to survive, and that only the "Athene" within us can effect the reconciliation. But how are we as individuals to bring to birth this reconciling symbol? Orestes in the play makes a quick journey to the city of Athene, which is passed over in silence. For each of us, however, who has identified with the Apollonian point of view, it is a long and difficult road, demanding a searching honesty and courage. The first step is surely to rid ourselves of the idea that we have outgrown the law of "an eye for an eye." We have to expose the delusion that, to forgive our enemies in accord with Christian ethic, it is only necessary to behave in an outwardly civilized manner, without bothering about what our repressed fury is doing. Every time we are hurt or angry or resentful toward a person, a circumstance or even a material thing, a desire to inflict an equivalent hurt is born, however unconscious we may be of it. We have suffered a little death and the desire to kill follows, for it is the nature of the psyche to seek always a restored balance. Demands refused, efforts frustrated, humiliations real or imagined, all breed the desire to effect a small "cleansing," as Clytemnestra did in her rage. But the new injury implies another, and so on without end. The fact that the injury is unseen merely increases its force. Husband, wife, children or friends can be driven by this hidden revenge into all manner of darkness.

The Christian answer is to turn the other cheek, but if we stop there we miss the whole meaning of Christ's message and only fall more deeply into this deadly menace of peace by repression. If we turn the other cheek, we are not thereby released from the law of the psyche, which demands a death for a death. It is better to have a blazing row than imagine this. The true "turning of the other cheek" is the full recognition of this law together with the willingness to accept the necessary death *within ourselves*, which is the only way to prevent its infliction on someone else, whether consciously or unconsciously. This is the whole answer as we see it in the life and death of Christ. "One jot or one tittle," he said, "shall in no wise pass from the law until all be fulfilled." This law of a death for a death is to be fulfilled by the injured individual himself, by one's recognition of the fact that the other one's guilt is also in a deep sense one's own, and by one's consent, in the midst of perhaps legitimate resentment, to pay the price, to die a little to the demand for justification and immunity. We may imagine for a moment how Clytemnestra might have seen Agamemnon as part of herself, not repressing her desire to kill him, but recognizing it on a deeper level as the desire to wipe out her *own* guilt, which is the root of all revenge. Actually the things she hated him for were precisely her own sins. She, too, had a lover; she too "murdered" inwardly her son and her daughter and was caught in an overweening pride. Jung has written of capital punishment that it is an assuaging, on a collective level, of each person's unconscious guilt for his own will to murder. The only end to this chain of blood for blood is in the individual's willingness to pay with his own blood for every injury he sustains. This and this only is the way to the discovery of the Athene within, the power that can meet the furies of the unconscious with love, and so discover in the heart of the fury itself the great nourishing, life-giving power of the all-forgiving Mother within.

Notes

Chapter One

1. Projection means a throwing out. Psychic contents of which we are unconscious are inevitably experienced as existing outside ourselves in some other person or fact of the environment.

2. *I Ching*, Richard Wilhelm version, trans. Cary F. Baynes, Bollingen Series XIX (New York, 1967), pp. 386–390.

3. C. G. Jung, *The Collected Works of C. G. Jung*, trans. R. F. C. Hull, Bollingen Series XX (New York, 1958), p. 416.

4. Elizabeth Jenkins, *Jane Austen: A Biography* (London, 1938), p. 363.

5. *The Complete Poems of Emily Dickinson*, ed. Thomas H. Johnson (Boston: Little, Brown & Co., 1966), p. vii.

6. *The Spirit in Man, Art, and Literature*, Bollingen Series XX, Vol. 15 (Princeton, 1971), p. 102.

Chapter Two

1. C. G. Jung, *The Collected Works of C. G. Jung*, trans. R. F. C. Hull, Bollingen Series XX (Princeton: Princeton University Press, 1950–79), vol. 18, pp. 280–81.

2. Jung, *The Collected Works*, vol. 10, p. 304.

3. *The Cloud of Unknowing*, ed. William Johnston (Garden City: Image Books, 1973), p. 50.

4. Jung, *Memories, Dreams, Reflections*, ed. Aniela Jaffe, trans. Richard and Clara Winston (New York: Pantheon Books, A Division of Random House, Inc., 1961), pp. 353–354.

5. Jung, *The Collected Works*, vol. 10, p. 279.

6. Jung, *The Collected Works*, vol. 9, p. 92.

7. *The Cloud of Unknowing*, pp. 16–17.

Chapter Three

1. Laurens Van der Post, *Patterns of Renewal,* Pendle Hill Pamphlet no. 121, 1962, p. 47.

2. T. S. Eliot, *The Four Quartets* (London: Faber & Faber), 1944, p. 42.

3. *I Ching,* Richard Wilhelm version, trans. Cary F. Baynes, Bollingen Series XIX (New York, 1967).

4. Eliot, *The Four Quartets.*

5. *Ibid.,* p. 44.

Chapter Four

1. The quotations in this chapter from C. G. Jung and C. Kerenyi are taken from *Introduction to a Science of Mythology,* trans. R. F. C. Hull (London: Routledge & Kegan Paul Ltd), 1951.

Chapter Five

1. English novelist and poet, friend of C. S. Lewis and J. R. Tolkien.

Chapter Six

1. Charles Williams, *Taliessin through Logres* (London: Oxford University Press, 1954 ed.).

2. *Ibid.,* p. 44.

3. *Ibid.*

4. *Ibid.*

5. *Ibid.*

6. *Ibid.,* p. 45.